D0039714

Lengthen
Your Smile

Lengthen Your Smile

A Year's Supply of Stories
for Latter-day Saints

Richard Nash

Deseret Book Company
Salt Lake City, Utah

To Laurie, my best friend

Library of Congress Cataloging-in-Publication Data

Lengthen your smile / [compiled] by Richard Nash.
   p.   cm.
  Includes index.
  ISBN 1-57345-046-4 (pb)
  1. Church of Jesus Christ of Latter-day Saints—Humor.
2. Mormon Church—Humor. 3. Mormons—Humor.
4. Church of Jesus Christ of Latter-day Saints—Anecdotes.
5. Mormon Church—Anecdotes. 6. Mormons—Anecdotes.
I. Nash, Richard, 1957–   .
BX8638.L57   1996
289.3'32—dc20   96-19527
                                     CIP

Printed in the United States of America

10 9   8   7   6   5   4   3   2   1

EXERCISE IS A PRIORITY to Ardeth G. Kapp, former general president of the Young Women. So is keeping up with her age group. "I heard the other day of a lady much older than I was who had completed fifty push-ups that very morning," said Sister Kapp. "That was distressing to me until I learned that she had begun them a year ago!"

Mᴀᴛᴛʜᴇᴡ Cᴏᴡʟᴇʏ ᴡᴀs ᴀ ɢʀᴇᴀᴛ ғʀɪᴇɴᴅ to the downtrodden. Instead of chiding them for where they were, he praised them for where they were going. One brother—"the worst man I ever knew," said Brother Cowley—bounced back from legal and family problems and said his goal was to go to the temple. Only his addiction to tobacco stood in the way.

"Well, he is headed in the right direction," Brother Cowley reported in a stake conference address. "Now, if he can get from Kools to cedar bark and from cedar bark to nothing he will be all right."

· JANUARY 3 ·

ANTI-MORMON FEELINGS RAN STRONG and deep in the southern states in the 1880s, when J. Golden Kimball was a young missionary there. He learned many lessons on his mission—one of them when his companion was saying a long prayer at the end of a meeting.

"When he said, 'Amen,' we looked back, and there were four men . . . with guns on their shoulders," Elder Kimball said forty years later in a conference address. "I said to my companion, 'That is another lesson; from this time on in the South, I shall pray with one eye open.'"

ON JANUARY 4, 1896—the day Utah became a state—President Wilford W. Woodruff sent a telegram to Frank Cannon, the son of Apostle George Q. Cannon, saying, "It is the will of the Lord that your father shall be elected senator from Utah. We want you to tell us how to bring it about."

Brother Frank answered with some frankness. "President Woodruff," he responded, "you have received the revelation on the wrong point. You do not need a voice from heaven to convince anyone that my father is worthy to go to the Senate, but you will need a revelation to tell how he is to get there."

A MAN WHO'D BEEN DRINKING walked into an LDS meetinghouse in the summer of 1996 in Salt Lake City's Avenues district, near the center of the city, and sought out the bishop. During their visit, the man asked for Church assistance—and shared a genealogical note designed to fortify his request. "My grandfather," said the inebriated brother, "was Shpencer W. Kimball."

"Then who's your father?" asked the nimble bishop.

"N. Eldon Tanner," said the man.

IN TALKING ABOUT HOW THE TRULY pure in heart will receive the word of God, Orson F. Whitney reported a conversation he'd had with a Book of Mormon skeptic. The man asked if the Lord used good grammar. Yes, said the apostle. Then why, the man asked, did the Book of Mormon contain a certain grammatical error?

"That," said Elder Whitney, "was left there just to keep you out of the Church."

GEORGE ALBERT SMITH SPENT a night in southern Utah with a family that wasn't active in the Church. When President Smith knelt at his chair and prayed before breakfast, the family's six-year-old boy was awestruck—and confused. "Daddy," said the boy when the prophet stood up, "what was that man saying to the chair?"

JON M. HUNTSMAN, A CLOSE FRIEND and neighbor of Howard W. Hunter, remembered when he and his family accompanied President Hunter on a trip to Guatemala. Brother Huntsman and his sons decided to climb the face of one of the country's steepest pyramids. "I'll see you when you return," said the aged apostle, who had visited the area before and knew there was an easier way to the summit.

"When we got toward the top and pulled ourselves up over the last step, there sitting on this big grassy knoll at the top was President Hunter," said Brother Huntsman. "As soon as he saw our heads emerge he said, 'What took you so long to get here?'"

BRIGHAM YOUNG BELIEVED THERE was a place in the Church for lightheartedness and humor.

When he received a letter from an angry woman who wanted her name removed from the rolls of the Church, he sent this reply: "Madam . . . I have this day examined the records of baptism for the remission of sins in the church . . . and not being able to find [your name] recorded therein, I was saved the necessity of erasing your name therefrom. You may therefore consider that your sins have not been remitted you and you can enjoy the benefits thereof."

BYU PROFESSOR TRUMAN MADSEN once asked Elder Richard L. Evans, "How do you account for your composure, your serenity of soul, under the frenetic schedule you must keep?" Elder Evans's answer: "Exhaustion!"

IN 1975, ON A TRIP TO Thatcher, Arizona—where Spencer W. Kimball had lived until his call to be an apostle—the prophet was welcomed warmly by old friends and family members. His sister Alice greeted him with a kiss, milled about with the other guests, then approached President Kimball again and gave him another kiss on the cheek. "Did I kiss you already?" she asked.

"The first time must not have impressed you much," replied her brother.

JOSEPH FIELDING SMITH AND his third wife, Jessie Evans Smith, lived in an apartment within a few hundred feet of his office in the Church Office Building. One day Sister Smith, who loved to tease her husband, called to say she was watching him through a pair of binoculars—and she wanted to know about the mysterious woman who was there with him.

"There is no woman in my office," President Smith said. "Oh, yes there is," retorted his wife.

The prophet came clean. "Jessie, I must confess," he said. "You've caught me cold!" On a pedestal near his desk was a bust of his great-grandmother, Lucy Mack Smith.

IN A STAKE CONFERENCE, J. Golden Kimball was presenting the names of the Church and stake officers to be sustained. The list was long, and as J. Golden read on he could tell the congregation had almost completely tuned him out. Such inattention was new to J. Golden, so he set about to correct it: "It has been proposed," he said, "that Mount Nebo be moved from its present site in Juab County and be placed on the Utah-Idaho border. All in favor, make it manifest."

JAMES L. PARKIN, a former stake president in Salt Lake City, told the following story in stake conference about his first trip to the Utah State Prison.

President Parkin said he had recently returned from his mission and was playing in an industrial basketball league against a prison team. Several factors contributed to the prison team's competitive edge, President Parkin recalled: Their fans were extremely partisan, and their players were very aggressive. "And they always had the home court advantage," he said.

· JANUARY 15 ·

Aす a college student, Elaine S. McKay discovered one source of a General Authority's strength. She was seated in the Salt Lake Tabernacle with her college roommate, who was a daughter of Ezra Taft Benson, and her roommate's five brothers and sisters. When Elder Benson was announced as the next speaker, Sister McKay watched him walk toward the podium. "He was a big man, well over six feet tall," she wrote. "He was a man with a Ph.D., a man internationally known as the United States Secretary of Agriculture, a special witness of the Lord, . . . one who had addressed audiences throughout the world."

As she watched him, a hand touched her arm. "A little girl leaned toward me and whispered, 'Pray for dad.'"

She passed the message down the row—and never forgot it. "I have come to believe," she said, "that is the most important message a family can share."

· 15 ·

· JANUARY 16 ·

FORTY YEARS AGO IN THE OLD Deseret Gym, a member of the Quorum of the Twelve sat by himself in the foggy peace of the steam bath. After some time, the door opened; a young boy, only eight or nine, came in and sat near the apostle in the thick steam. The boy moved nearer to the apostle and watched him intently.

"Mister," said the boy eventually, "I think I know who you are.

"I think," he continued, "you are one of the apostles of the Church. I think you are the one who travels all over the ocean on big boats and little boats and all kinds of airplanes—and you are the one who never gets sick or hurt in any wrecks." The apostle agreed with that job description.

"Do you know why it is you don't ever get killed or get hurt?" asked the boy.

"No," said the apostle. "Why is that?"

"Because I pray for you," said the boy.

WHEN N. ELDON TANNER was a stake president in Canada, he and two companions picked up a hitchhiker. After making himself comfortable in the back seat, the man asked if President Tanner would mind if he smoked. Not at all, the stake president said—but only if the man could name one good reason why he should smoke. "I will go farther than that," President Tanner then added. "If you can give me a good reason why you should smoke, I will smoke with you."

Twenty minutes later the future apostle looked back at his rider and asked if he was going to smoke. "No," said the man. "Why not?" asked President Tanner. "I can't think of a good reason why I should," said the man.

ON A BOAT TO HAWAII IN 1950, George Albert Smith departed with a flourish from his usual diet of steamed wheat, boiled eggs, bread, and milk. At dinner one night, he ordered roast capon in burgundy. "Papa, you don't want that; it's been cooked in burgundy," said his daughter.

President Smith persisted: "I don't care if it's been cooked in Australia!"

AFTER A BYU DEVOTIONAL in which Joseph Fielding Smith not only talked but sang, President Smith wasn't surprised to hear that some members of the audience had wept during his performance. "My singing," he said, "is enough to make anybody cry."

WAYNE PETERSON, a regional representative from Holladay, Utah, told the story of a young LDS girl in Oakland, California, who answered the phone one night and told the caller her parents weren't home.

They were doing temple work, said the girl, whose interpretation of temple work wasn't yet very refined. "Last week they did sealings. Tonight they're doing walls."

D. ARTHUR HAYCOCK, longtime personal secretary to five presidents of the Church, remembers that Joseph Fielding Smith liked two kinds of pie: hot and cold.

WHILE HE WAS AN APOSTLE, Heber J. Grant persisted in his determination to learn to sing. A close friend who had heard his reedy practices gave him some advice in a letter. "If you can learn to sing, nothing need discourage anybody," the friend wrote. "But the fact that success ultimately must be reached by traveling along the borderland of ridicule makes the task a difficult and delicate one, particularly for an apostle, who, unlike the ordinary musical crank, cannot afford to cultivate his thorax at the expense of his reputation as a man of judgment."

SHARLENE WELLS, a twenty-year-old Sunday School teacher and BYU coed, was crowned Miss America in 1984 after the previous year's winner lost the crown following the printing of some scandalous photos.

The press had a heyday with the impeccable background of the Mormon Miss America. One cartoon showed the publisher of a girlie magazine talking on the phone, saying, "Silhouettes of her sipping a milkshake with Marie Osmond and two straws? That's all you can get?"

ONE OF JOSEPH FIELDING SMITH'S sisters once found him in his office on a holiday, immersed in his work. She needled him for not taking the day off. "All my days are off," he replied. She said he should be home, taking a nap, and named former Church leaders who had napped religiously. "George Albert Smith, Stephen L Richards, and J. Reuben Clark always did, so you can, too," she said.

"Yes," said the prophet, "and look where they are now!"

LEGEND HAS IT THAT IF YOU WRAP your arms around an old column that stands in Oaxaca, Mexico, you can count the number of years left in your life by measuring the space between the tips of your fingers. In 1952, two General Authorities tried it: Spencer W. Kimball and Bruce R. McConkie. The diminutive Elder Kimball found he could look forward to sixteen more years, but Elder McConkie's long arms wrapped completely around the column, and even overlapped a little.

Said Elder Kimball to Elder McConkie: "You're already dead—but don't know it."

MEMBERS OF EACH RISING GENERATION are stronger and more faithful than many of those who came before. For those who don't believe it, remember the story about a young man who dreamed one night about his father. The next morning the father asked his boy what he had dreamed.

"I dreamed I was climbing a ladder to heaven, and on the way up I had to write one of my sins on each step of the ladder," said the boy.

"And where did I come into your dream?" asked the father.

"When I was going up," the boy said, "I met you coming down for more chalk."

WHEN DANIEL HESS WAS A young sailor in the U.S. Navy, many of his boot camp bunkmates were men with low standards and foul language. One day Dan and a friend were sitting in their barracks when one of the roughest men in their unit stormed into the room in and cut loose with a barrage of filthy language, some of which was aimed directly at the Lord.

"My friend looked at me and said, 'Dan, we're not going to take that, are we?' I thought about it for a minute, and finally said, 'I guess not,'" said Brother Hess years later. "So I stepped out in front of the man as he came down the rows of beds, and I told him that I loved the Savior and that he couldn't say those things about him."

The vulgar sailor stopped to think. "In the end he apologized," said Brother Hess. "I'd like to think, for his sake, that it wasn't just because I happened to be the camp boxing champion."

JOSEPH FIELDING SMITH once said his Church service dated back to the Saints' early years in Utah. "My first Church assignment was to accompany Brigham Young to the dedication of the St. George Temple." He paused while his audience worked to calculate how long ago that must have been—and how old that would make President Smith.

Then he added a detail: "I was just one year old then."

STANDING UP FOR YOUR BELIEFS is important—if your beliefs are worth standing up for. Don't be like the boy who said, "I have a family history of courage and backbone. My father was even put in jail for his beliefs . . . He believed the night watchman was asleep."

BLAINE WILCOX, A DENTIST in Salt Lake City and a former bishop, was asked to give a talk in sacrament meeting. At the beginning of his talk, he explained that he'd been asked to speak roughly eight or nine minutes. "That might be hard," he said. "I haven't known anyone who could speak roughly for that long since I was in the Navy."

Swear not at all," we read in Matthew. Daniel S. Hess provides an example. "My father was a farmer and put in long, hard days of labor, much of it with animals," he wrote. "If any earthly trial I know of can drive a man to profanity, it is working with animals." But Brother Hess's father did not profane—even in the most trying circumstances.

The elder Hess was milking a fevered cow one day. "Father had cracked his ribs not long before, and they were excruciatingly painful," said Dan. "As if that weren't enough, the cow in her sickness suddenly collapsed and fell right on top of him. It would have been a funny sight if it hadn't been for his white-faced agony."

The farmer struggled to escape from under the cow, and once he was able to stand, got the cow back to her feet. "Although he was sick with pain, he didn't call the cow any bad names," said his son. "He ran his hand gently along her side and said, 'You poor dear, I'm sorry you're so sick.'"

IN THE CALIFORNIA SAN DIEGO MISSION in the mid-1970s, a young, new missionary—a mild-mannered Idaho farm boy six and a half feet tall—knocked on the door of a man whose hostility equaled his size.

The man didn't want to listen to the message of the young elder and his companion, and he began to mock them and their beliefs. The elders started to leave, but the man followed them, stepping out from behind his screen door onto the porch. "You don't even know there's a God," he said angrily, gesturing skyward. "If there is a God, have him strike me down this moment."

Without warning, the man was knocked backward into his house, right through his screen door. The missionaries beat a hasty retreat down the sidewalk.

"I remember what my folks told me before I came on my mission," said the elder from Idaho. "Never ask the Lord to do anything you're not willing to do yourself."

WHATSOEVER YE DO," WROTE PAUL to the Colossians, "do it heartily." David O. McKay knew that. His enthusiasm for living never diminished, even after his health faded as his age advanced. When President McKay and his wife were both confined to wheelchairs, wrote a biographer, "they would good-humoredly challenge each other to 'a race to the elevator.'"

JACOB HAMBLIN WAS AN EARLY Mormon pioneer who was loved and respected by the Indians for his integrity. On one occasion in Southern Utah, Brother Hamblin sent his son to trade a pony to the Indians for some blankets. Brother Hamblin told his son that the pony was worth about three blankets, but the boy thought he could do better; he came home with six.

Brother Hamblin sent his son marching right back to the Indian village. "I knew it, I knew it," said an Indian upon the young man's return. "The boy's father sent him— three too many blankets."

ANY PARENT KNOWS THAT DISCIPLINE—and agency—are important, and that the two don't always peacefully coexist. Take the story of a salesman who came to a door on a sunny summer day. Inside the front door was a young man, his baseball mitt and hat right beside him as he sat on a piano bench and pounded out his practice scales.

"Say, boy, is your mother home?" asked the salesman.

"What do you think?" said the boy.

Waste not, want not," says the old adage. But what about when there's a fly in the ointment—or in the molasses?

"Wasty Jake Beecham" was an early southern Utah pioneer who earned his nickname as a boy for wasting molasses. One night at supper Jake's brother cried, "Ma, Jake's wasty! He picked a fly out of the 'lasses and never licked its legs off!"

STEPHEN L RICHARDS, who was a counselor to David O. McKay, said he always appreciated the Relief Society—except once. On his wedding day he reserved a prestigious and expensive hack, or horse-drawn carriage, to take him and his bride from the temple to their new home. "It was the first hack I had ever hired," he said. "I was quite proud to think I could get it to take my wife home after the marriage."

But when young Brother Richards greeted his bride at the temple gate, he found she was accompanied by an elderly Relief Society sister she'd met in the temple. "This sister lives two or three miles out on the way," said the new Sister Richards, "and I thought we could take her home."

"I don't remember," said President Richards over fifty years later, "whether she sat between us or not."

ONE MORNING, AS A YOUNG MOTHER did her housework, her three-year-old son followed her everywhere. He followed so closely that she kept stepping on him. She finally asked him what he was doing. He explained that his Primary teacher had told him he should walk in Jesus' footsteps. "But I can't see him," he said, "so I'm walking in yours."

At a RELIEF SOCIETY general conference in 1953, David O. McKay related an experience of the prominent educator Francis Wayland Parker. After a lecture, a woman asked Parker how soon she could start working on the education of her child.

"When will your child be born?" Parker asked.

"Born?" replied the woman. "Why, he is already five years old."

"My goodness, woman," said the educator, "don't stand here talking to me—hurry home. Already you have lost the best five years!"

A PROPHET, THE BIBLE SAYS, is without honor in his own country. And in other countries, he's sometimes without basic comfort.

On a ship to Japan during a world tour in 1920, the young apostle David O. McKay was so enthusiastically seasick that "it was good-bye to everything I had ever eaten since I was a babe on mother's knee," he wrote. "I am not sure I didn't even cross the threshold into the pre-existent state." And later, after journeying through the Middle East, Elder McKay added a postscript to a letter sent to his young son: "P.S. I accept as absolute facts every plague of Egypt named in the Bible, and add to them the 'plague of fleas,' which Moses forgot to mention."

ON A TRAIN TRIP TO A stake conference, Orson F. Whitney immersed himself so completely in his thoughts that he missed his stop and had to be driven back. He walked into stake conference late—in the middle of the opening hymn: "Ye Simple Souls Who Stray."

N. ELDON TANNER TOLD THE STORY of talking with his teenaged daughter before she went out for the evening. He instructed her to have a good time—and then, as she left, he added, "Behave yourself!"

"Well, Dad," said the daughter, "make up your mind!"

SEVERAL YEARS AGO THE YOUNG NIECE of Ardeth G. Kapp, former general president of the Young Women, was just old enough to not believe in Santa Claus but still young enough to be captivated by the magic of St. Nick's impending visit. The girl approached her mother for advice. "Mom," she asked, "is it okay if I believe just one more year?"

Suffrage, or giving women the right to vote, was popular in the Utah territory well before it caught on in the rest of the nation, but equal respect for the sexes was still sometimes a battle in pioneer times. Nancy Greene, whose family settled in Escalante's Potato Valley, remembered that one of her family's cows wouldn't let a man approach her. "If for any reason one of the men had to handle her, he would have to put on a woman's dress, apron, and sunbonnet," she said. "We children thought this very funny."

So, probably, did the cow.

Let me assure you, brethren, that some day you will have a personal priesthood interview with the Savior, himself," said David O. McKay in a 1965 talk to Church employees. "If you are interested, I will tell you the order in which he will ask you to account for your earthly responsibilities." Here, said President McKay, is what the Lord will ask:

1. He will want an accountability report about your relationship with your wife.

2. He will want an accountability report about each of your children.

3. He will want to know what you have done with the talents you were given.

4. He will want a summary of your activity in your Church assignments.

5. He will have no interest in how you earned your living, but he will ask whether you were honest in all your dealings.

6. He will ask for an accountability of what you have done to enhance your community, state, country, and the world.

DURING A TRIP TO THE EAST COAST while
World War I was raging in Europe, President
George Albert Smith paid a courtesy visit to
New York Governor Charles Whitman. The
two men, who had met earlier when President
Smith had given the governor a copy of the
Book of Mormon, had a pleasant conversation
late one night in the governor's den.

During their visit, as the two leaders discussed how the war would turn out, the governor expressed concern about the outcome—
but President Smith reassured him America
would be victorious. He turned to the corre-
sponding reference in Governor Whitman's
Book of Mormon to prove the point.

"I had not seen that," said the governor.

Responded the prophet: "You are not
doing a very good job reading your Book of
Mormon."

SPENCER W. KIMBALL WAS DETERMINED to earn his keep when he stayed at the home of a local stake president during a conference in Idaho in 1947. The apostle milked cows and did chores after the Saturday night meeting, then pitched in again early on Sunday before church. The stake president recounted Elder Kimball's diligence when he introduced the apostle during conference—and people were impressed.

"After the meeting," Elder Kimball wrote in his journal, "people came up to shake hands and said, 'When you come next time you can stay with us.'"

DURING A ROUND-THE-WORLD TRIP in 1921, David O. McKay was greeted by an enthusiastic, jubilant audience of Saints before a conference on a Polynesian island. Processional lines formed; the apostle and his party started to shake hands with each of the several hundred people in attendance. "Being pretty well-filled with the Maori spirit," he wrote, "we found ourselves not only shaking hands, but hongi-ing one by one [rubbing noses] and one after another.

"What an experience!" he recalled. "You who think Maori noses are all alike have never hongied a multitude!"

ONE DAY IN THE Church Administration Building, a young man walking behind Joseph Fielding Smith quickly stepped after the apostle to catch an elevator just as the door was sliding shut. Inside the elevator, the young man said he hoped the same thing would happen in the next life. "If I can catch the pearly gates before they close behind someone like you, I may make it," he said.

Elder Smith winked at him. "If I were you, my brother," he said, "I wouldn't count on it."

BETWEEN HIS TRAVELS and meetings, between visits with presidents and kings and ambassadors, Spencer W. Kimball filled his schedule with personal appointments with individual members of the Church. One small boy, who stepped into President Kimball's office in 1974 to shake the hand of the seventy-nine-year-old prophet, was very clear about the purpose of his visit. "I wanted to see you before you died," he said.

SOON AFTER BRIGHAM YOUNG opened a playhouse in Salt Lake City, some local boys—including some of his sons—caught the spirit of the stage. They wrote a play called *The Robbers of the Rocky Mountains* and started to produce it with some scenery they had filched from the prophet's barn.

Brother Brigham met with the boys, then sent a note to the manager of the Salt Lake Theatre. "These boys have a play," it said. "They call it *The Robbers of the Rocky Mountains.* I don't know much about the mountains, but they certainly made a clean job of my old barn. Give them a date at the Theatre."

POOR HEALTH AFFLICTED J. Golden Kimball as he grew older. "I thank God I do not feel as bad as I look," he said once.

One day he was examined by a young physician who didn't believe in God. After a brief theological discussion, the doctor told J. Golden that with only the Lord as his physician, he'd never get better. But J. Golden, as usual, had the last word. The young physician, he reported later, "was drowned last year, and I am still alive."

NOT LONG AFTER Spencer W. Kimball became president of the Church, someone asked him what he did for fun. He answered, with a twinkle in his eye, "Sleep!"

WHILE SPENCER W. KIMBALL was recovering from surgery on his larynx, one side effect significantly altered his lifestyle. "Insomnia is my trouble," he wrote in a letter. "Why, I couldn't even doze in sacrament meeting yesterday."

HUGH B. BROWN RECALLED the advice his mother gave him at a train station in Canada, in 1904, when he was leaving on a mission. "Do you remember when you were a little boy, you had bad dreams and would cry out, 'Mother, are you there?'? And I would say, 'Yes, son, I'm here, just turn over and go to sleep.' You always did, knowing I was near and that you didn't need to fear anymore.

"Always remember God is as close as you will let him be, and if you call out, 'Father, are you there?' there will come into your heart a feeling of his presence, and you will know you can depend on him."

"Many, many times since then, in the ensuing sixty or more years, I have cried out and asked, 'Father, are you there?'" Elder Brown said. "And always I have had the impression that he was mindful of me, was available to me, and would see me safely through."

Bryant S. Hinckley, the father of Gordon B. Hinckley, told a story in 1958 about two boys, aged seven and nine, who were playing together, building a toy car. One of them said, "Which do you think is the most fun, making or having?"

The other boy thought for a moment, looking at all the construction materials spread out around them. "Making!" he said.

"The creative instinct is deep in the human soul and its reward is satisfaction and joy," said Brother Hinckley. "The happiest people in the world are those who learn this lesson early."

DURING HIS TERM AS PRESIDENT of the British Mission, Hugh B. Brown met with a writer who'd been commissioned to write an exposé about the Church. As he began his research, the man met with Elder Brown, who asked if the man would spend thirty days researching the writings of Church leaders before he started to write. The man agreed. "I thought it only fair to warn him that if he spent thirty days . . . reading on Mormonism, he would ask for baptism," said Elder Brown.

"Why, the idea that I would become a Mormon is preposterous," replied the writer.

The man spent several weeks in a library, reading—and praying. Within thirty days, the writer sent Elder Brown a telegram. "I think you will be interested to know," he said, "that I am being baptized next Friday."

BRIGHAM YOUNG HAD SOME practical advice for a woman who complained to him that her husband had told her to go to hell: "Don't go."

J. GOLDEN KIMBALL SUFFERED from appendicitis fairly late in his life. While his physicians debated whether or not surgery was needed, he spent some time thinking his days on earth were reaching an end. "People said to me, 'Well, Brother Kimball, you needn't be afraid, you'll get justice.'

"'That,' I told them, 'is what I am afraid of.'"

AFTER BEING ARRESTED ON false charges and threatened with prison and a stiff fine, missionary Parley P. Pratt cooperated with his captors—until he ran out of patience.

One morning he told his guard he was leaving, then sprinted toward the nearby woods. Yelling and pointing at Elder Pratt, the man sent his big bulldog after the fleeing missionary. As the dog was about to catch him, Elder Pratt started mimicking its master's actions, yelling and pointing at the woods ahead of him. The dog ran right past him.

Said Elder Pratt, "Gaining the forest, I soon lost sight of the officer and the dog, and have not seen them since."

Truman Madsen and his wife, who presided over the New England mission, were in Boston's Harvard Square when six seminarians walked past in clerical robes. Sister Madsen approached them, asked if they knew anything about the Church, and wondered if they'd like to know more. "Of course not," they said. "We're preparing for the ministry."

But Sister Madsen was persistent. She invited them to the mission home on Thanksgiving. The seminarians refused.

However, Thanksgiving night, the mission home's doorbell rang, and there were four of the aspiring clerics. "They came in and we had a magnificent evening," said Brother Madsen.

For about six months they came back every chance they had. "They brought a different student with them each time until we knew twenty of them," said Brother Madsen. "Next fall one of them will be at BYU. He's the one we taught all six discussions."

BYU FOOTBALL COACH LaVELL EDWARDS is well-known for the dour demeanor he displays throughout his team's games. Win or lose, the coach's consistently stern sideline expression never changes.

But don't let the frown deceive you. Off the field, LaVell is known for his wit, warmth, and genuine goodness. "I've never not enjoyed myself," he said.

One of his friends—former BYU golf coach Karl Tucker—puts Edwards's expression into perspective. "LaVell's happy," he said. "He just forgot to tell his face."

WHO'S THE CAPTAIN OF YOUR SOUL: you or the circumstances that surround you? Do you act, as Nephi suggests, or are you acted upon?

The great American jurist Oliver Wendell Holmes created his own circumstances, even though he, like the rest of us, faced hardships. One of Judge Holmes's challenges was his size; he wasn't much more than five feet tall. But that was just his physical measurement.

Once, in a meeting of a large group of people, Holmes was obviously the shortest person in the room. "Don't you feel strange," asked an insensitive colleague, "being so short among all these taller men?"

"Yes," he said. "I feel like a dime among pennies."

FLEE—DON'T STROLL, don't meander—from idolatry, said the apostle Paul. Hartman Rector, Jr., repeated that idea in a 1972 conference talk with a lesson he learned during his twenty-six years as a pilot in the U.S. Navy. "Flat-hatting"—or seeing how close you could fly to the trees—was a popular game, but it was dangerous, and it was against Navy rules. So to the Navy's commandment— "Thou shalt not fly thy airplane in the trees"—Elder Rector added a rule of his own: "Thou shalt not fly thy airplane closer than 5,000 feet to the trees."

That's a good way to deal with all the commandments, he advised.

"When you are flying just high enough to miss the trees and your engine coughs once," he said, "you are in the trees."

DORALEE DURHAM MADSEN—who, with her husband, Richard, has ten children—drafted a list of "family joys." Included among her entries are

• Joy is reading the scriptures with the family and having the two-year-old bring his own Sesame Street book to scripture study.

• Joy is going to the hospital once, twice, or ten times to welcome a new little spirit into the world, and a sister asking, "Why don't they invent a new-baby-smell perfume?"

• Joy is sharing the flu because you wanted to share your drink with your sister.

• Joy is being told by a four-year-old that her daddy's name is "Bishop."

• Joy is losing the election at the same school where your sister won and having the winning sister cry harder than the loser.

What's on your list of family joys?

SHARLENE WELLS, 1984's Miss America, is talented, poised, and physically fit, according to her family and friends. She's also human. "She eats like a horse," said Randy Boothe, who was director of BYU's Young Ambassadors when Sharlene toured with the group. "I've never seen a girl who could put away more at McDonald's than Sharlene."

But she didn't eat thoughtlessly. "We were eating at this one restaurant," he remembered, "and she turned to me—completely serious—and asked, 'Which do you think has the least calories, chocolate cake or chocolate pudding?'"

DARLENE CURTIS WAS STUDYING to be a nun when her brother joined The Church of Jesus Christ of Latter-day Saints. At first her family disowned him, but gradually other members of the family, including her mother, began investigating the Church.

"My sister had been in a convent for almost three years and her husband attended a Catholic seminary for four years, preparing for the priesthood," Darlene recounts. "In an attempt to prevent mother from joining the Mormon church, they looked into it. I attended their baptism and was impressed."

Eventually, Darlene's parents and five of her six brothers and sisters joined the Church. And, after twelve years of service as a nun, so did she.

ARDETH G. KAPP once visited a second-grade classroom where the teacher told the story of two men: Mr. Brown, who was kind and friendly, and Mr. Black, who was angry and mean. "How many of you would like to be a neighbor to Mr. Brown?" asked the teacher. Every hand in the room went up.

And who would want to be neighbors with Mr. Black?

A little boy in a faded shirt raised his hand. Some of the other students started to titter, but the boy was resolute. His hand stayed up. The teacher asked the boy to explain his choice, and he said, "Well, I'd like Mr. Black to be my neighbor, because if he was, my mom would make a cake for me to take to him, and then he wouldn't be that way anymore."

The room fell silent. "Everyone felt something wonderful that they couldn't explain," said Sister Kapp. "A little child broke the silence like a benediction: 'Oh, I wish I'd said that!'"

DAVID O. MCKAY GREW UP in a spiritual home, and he and his wife, Emma Ray Riggs, created one after they married. One of their sons, while still a small boy, reflected his background one day when he watched a hired man who was hanging wallpaper. "When you are a man, would you like to be a painter and paper-hanger?" asked the man.

"No, sir," said the boy. "I should like to be a Twelve Apostle."

ONE SUNDAY, A BUSY BISHOP in a meeting-house's crowded hall stopped to help a small boy who sat in the hallway, crying. "He sat right down on the floor and held the little boy close until the crying subsided and the boy was able to explain what was wrong," recounts former general Primary president Michaelene P. Grassli. Then the boy and the bishop stood up and walked together, hand in hand, to where the boy belonged. "I sense that the Savior would have done that, too."

MARVIN J. ASHTON TOLD THE STORY of a happy, positive, highly respected woman. "She was a delight to be around because she seemed to love life and people to the fullest," he said. "One day I said to her, 'You are such a joy to all of us. What is your secret?'"

The woman said one word had changed her life.

"And what was that word?" Elder Ashton asked.

"Malignant!" said the woman. "The doctor said that word to me and told me I had a limited time to live," she continued. "I had a choice. I could make everyone miserable or I could try to make others happy. On my knees I realized that I had one day at a time, just as everyone else has. I was able to see things I had never seen. My husband, my children, each person took on a beauty you can't believe. I know that life is a gift whether it be a day or a year, and I intend to enjoy my gift to the maximum."

Don't worry; be happy" is not just a twentieth-century philosophy. According to an early Mormon leader, it was expressed in different words by the Prophet Joseph Smith. The prophet had stretched out under a shade tree one day to relax, and was doing very well at it when a hunter walked past and reprimanded him for his sedate manner.

Brother Joseph responded by asking the man if he kept his bow strung up tight when he wasn't hunting. Of course not, said the man. Why not? asked the prophet. Because the weapon would lose its elasticity and thus its potency, said the hunter.

"The prophet said it was just so with his mind," recounted the brother who witnessed the incident. "He did not want it strung up all the time."

NEAR THE TURN OF THE CENTURY, some Saints in one of the Church's stakes supported the Word of Wisdom so zealously they decided to supplement that revelation with an additional list of items they'd avoid. When their list was drafted, they showed it to J. Golden Kimball, who'd been assigned to visit their stake conference.

But when J. Golden read the list, he wasn't impressed; he was mortified. "Blankedty-blank!" he said. "Soup will go next!"

IN THE 1950s, MARVIN J. ASHTON was assigned to visit a stake in Canada that was presided over by N. Eldon Tanner. A stake meeting had been set for 7:00 P.M. one night, but when 7:00 P.M. came, the two church leaders were the only ones in the chapel.

Elder Ashton checked his watch and asked, "President Tanner, what do you suggest we do?"

President Tanner gave an answer all presiding officers should keep in mind. "You're here," he said to Elder Ashton. "I'm here. It's seven o'clock. Let's start."

WHEN PAUL NASH WAS BAPTIZED in the warm, deep waters of the baptismal font at his Salt Lake City stake center, his newfound spirituality was eclipsed by his third-grade practicality. "Paul," said an awestruck younger cousin after the service, "all your sins have been washed away!"

"I know," he said. "Plus I don't have to have a bath tonight!"

WHEN ARDETH G. KAPP was a teenager, she stayed out one night past her curfew and was mortified to have her father show up in the middle of a party to take her home.

Several years later, on the way home from another party, Sister Kapp and some friends stalled their car on a snowy road in the middle of a Canadian blizzard. The young people wondered whether they'd freeze to death. Then one friend turned to Sister Kapp and said, "How long do you think it will be before your dad will get here?"

It wasn't long at all. "One time I wanted to die because my dad came after me," Sister Kapp said. "Another time my friends and I lived because he came."

Truman Madsen, always an enthusiastic missionary, caught a cab one day in Montreal. As they traveled, Brother Madsen asked the driver if he loved his wife, and the man said that he did. "And I could see his eyes in the rear-view mirror, and I knew that he meant it," said Brother Madsen.

"Then I said (this is terribly presumptuous, but I'm bold with cab drivers), 'Are you faithful to your wife?'"

"Yes, sir!" said the cab driver.

Why? "Because I love her," said the man.

When the cab reached its destination, Brother Madsen said, "You'll forget me. But here's my card. You just remember that tonight you talked to the only man you may ever meet who could have told you how you could have your wife forever."

The result? "He contacted the Church that next Sunday," said Brother Madsen. "They have joined the Church. My wife and I expect to go to the temple with them."

AN ACTOR FROM THE EAST came to Utah to perform in the Salt Lake Theatre. During his stay, he fell in love with Sara Alexander, a young LDS girl, an orphan whose guardian was Brigham Young. The actor asked Brother Brigham to grant him Miss Alexander's hand in marriage.

"Young man," replied the prophet, "I have seen you attempt Richard III and Julius Caesar with fair success, but I advise you not to aspire to Alexander."

WHEN HE WAS JUST SEVENTEEN, Matthew Cowley was called on a mission to New Zealand. He was assigned to a town called Judea, and at the end of his first Church meeting there, a woman who spoke English asked him if he understood what had happened during the meeting. "I could not understand a word," he said.

"Well," said the sister, "you were called and sustained as secretary of the Relief Society of the Judea Branch."

Years later Elder Cowley said, "I made up my mind right there and then . . . to get the gift of the Maori language."

ARDETH G. KAPP, former general president
of the Young Women, relates how someone
once asked Spencer W. Kimball how he ever
relaxed enough to get to sleep at night with
all the responsibilities he shouldered. Did the
prophet count sheep? "No," said President
Kimball. "I talk to the Shepherd."

HAROLD B. LEE RECEIVED A NOTE from an amused Primary president soon after he became the Church's eleventh president. She wrote that when she held up his picture in Primary, it sparked a jolt of recognition in one of her young friends. "I know him," said the child. "We sing about him all the time in church: Reverent Lee, Quiet Lee . . ."

NO ONE WHO IS STRIVING TO DO his duty in the Church should be shocked when any call comes," said Marvin J. Ashton.

Shocked, no. Surprised, yes. The dedicated but demure wife of one Latter-day Saint leader wrote this after her husband completed a term as president of the local Rotary Club: "It was a very pleasant experience but I really do not crave publicity. I am satisfied to go quietly my own way. . . . I never expect to come as near the center of the stage again."

Who said it? Camilla Kimball—about forty years before her husband, Spencer, was called to be president of the Church.

AFTER A MISSION TO THE SOUTH in the 1880s—where several of his fellow missionaries were shot to death and many more were beaten, lashed with leather straps, and otherwise persecuted—J. Golden Kimball knew both courage and fear. "I never was afraid of a mob in the southern states when I had the Spirit of God," he said years later in general conference, "but I was scared pretty nearly to death after the Spirit left."

I^T'S SURPRISING THE THINGS you can learn while teaching. The teacher of a youth Sunday School class told his students the story of David and Goliath, then asked the class to name the moral of the story.

One student's response: "Duck!"

THREE-YEAR-OLD CHRISSY STORNETTA had sugar diabetes—and faith. In the grocery store with her mother, she pointed out all the treats she couldn't eat—cookies, candy, doughnuts, and more—and then proclaimed, "Mommy, I can eat this when I'm resurrected, can't I?"

DURING A SUNDAY MEETING when Spencer W. Kimball was a stake leader in Arizona, he noticed seven small boys sitting on the front row, facing him as he sat on the stand. The boys were acting very strangely. They crossed their legs in unison; then uncrossed them. All together, they brushed their hair; they leaned forward; they leaned back. "It all seemed so strange," President Kimball thought, until he realized they were mimicking him.

"That day," he said, "I learned the lesson of my life: That we who are in positions of authority must be careful indeed, because others watch us and find in us their examples."

SET GOALS, COUNSELED Elder Marvin J. Ashton; know where you're going and how you're going to get there. At a Young Women's fireside in 1981, he told the story of a man who jumped into a taxicab and breathlessly told the driver, "Hurry, hurry, I'm late!" The cabbie hit the gas and the cab shot out into traffic and roared down the street—until the passenger said, "Oh, I forgot to tell you where to go."

"I know," said the cabbie, "but we are surely making good time."

SPENCE KINARD, FORMER VOICE of *Music and the Spoken Word,* told the story of a trip he took with the Tabernacle Choir to Munich, Germany. At a rest stop, the choir members had an hour and a half to sightsee and shop before they had to catch their train. As the allotted time ran out, one choir member approached Brother Kinard on the street and asked, "Excuse me—do you speak English? I am a member of the Tabernacle Choir and I'm lost."

"I didn't have the heart to tell her I was Spence Kinard," he said.

PHILIP SONNTAG, WHEN HE WAS A SEALER in the Salt Lake Temple, performed a marriage in which he gave great marital—and fire prevention—advice. He counseled the new bride to fill a bucket with water and keep it within reach. "The only time anyone should ever yell at anyone else in your house is if there's a fire," said Brother Sonntag, "and then the bucket of water will come in handy.

"And if there's no fire and your husband ever raises his voice at you," he told the bride, "dump the water on him."

AT THE SITE OF A NEW CHAPEL, two local Church leaders held the arms of David O. McKay to assist him as a party of Church officials walked up a hill. The prophet, who was then over ninety years old, halted after several steps.

"Brethren, I don't mind helping one of you climb this hill," he told his assistants, "but I can't carry you both."

· APRIL 1 ·

ONE NIGHT IN 1849, Jacob Hamblin had a vivid and stirring dream. He acted on it the next day. He walked to the door of a widow in Council Bluffs, Iowa, and said, "My name is Jacob Hamblin; I was impressed to come to your home and ask you to be my wife." Her answer: "I am Rachel Judd, and am willing to marry you, but it will be impossible for us to have children."

"My name is Jacob, yours is Rachel," he replied. "We will have two sons and shall name them Joseph and Benjamin." They did—and three daughters as well.

Heber C. Kimball, the apostle and counselor to Brigham Young, was also the father of J. Golden Kimball, and he and his son shared some of the same vocabulary. Someone once asked Elder Kimball—who had suffered much at the hands of anti-Mormon mobs in the early days of the Church—if he prayed for those who persecuted the Saints. "Sure I'll pray for our enemies!" he said. "I pray they may all go to hell!"

A MISSION PRESIDENT once asked his missionaries in their interviews: When did you have your last spiritual experience? The answers were illuminating—especially the response of one committed, spiritual young elder who said his most recent spiritual experience had happened just that morning.

"What happened this morning?" asked the mission president.

"I prayed," said the missionary.

Ruth B. Wright, former second counselor in the general presidency of the Primary, told the story of a Primary teacher who gathered her class around her and told them how special they were and how well they were doing. "You have learned so many things," said the teacher. "You have learned to sit reverently and listen to our lessons. Why, you can even say your own prayers!"

"Well, of course," replied one young boy. "I've already been on this earth five years!"

MATTHEW COWLEY ENCOURAGED local Church leaders to keep track of ward members' talents so those in need would have access to the right kinds of help. For example, Brother Cowley said, in addition to being a lawyer he'd worked as a cook. "Nothing would please me more than to have my bishop call me up and say, 'Brother Cowley, this is an emergency; we have a sister up here with a family of children; the husband's an invalid. . . . How about coming up and cooking the dinner for the next three nights?'

"I don't know how long that invalid would last," said Brother Cowley, "but I'd be glad to go up."

D<small>URING THE</small> 1940<small>S</small>, <small>THE</small> P<small>RIMARY</small> led a massive, Churchwide fund-raising campaign to help build Primary Children's Hospital. The campaign included a "Buy-a-Brick" drive, in which Primary children were asked to contribute a dime to buy each of the hospital's bricks. The drive raised over $20,000, which was used to buy 203,303 bricks.

During a tour of the new hospital, a little hand pulled at the skirt of the Primary board member who was leading a group of children. "Lady," asked a small boy, "can you tell me which is my brick?"

Asked what he thought of young women wearing makeup, J. Golden Kimball was typically practical—and typically direct.

"We paint our houses, don't we?" he said. "I guess a girl is entitled to as much privilege as a house."

・ APRIL 8 ・

SPENCER W. KIMBALL TOLD THE STORY of
how he admired Harold B. Lee, who was his
mentor and friend in the Quorum of the
Twelve. Over the course of their friendship,
President Kimball noted many times the great
skills of President Lee, and told him many
times that he wished he could do things—play
the organ, give talks, solve problems, etc.,
etc.—as well as President Lee did.

"One day," President Kimball said, "I
guess Harold had had enough. He stopped,
put his hands on his hips, and looking me
straight in the eye, said, 'Spencer, the Lord
doesn't want you to be a Harold B. Lee. All
he wants is for you to be the best Spencer W.
Kimball you can be.'

"Ever since then," said President Kimball,
"I have just tried to be the best Spencer W.
Kimball I can be."

MARK TWAIN AND A PARTY traveling with him through the West gained an audience one day with Brigham Young. The "Mormon king," as the author called him, "seemed a quiet, kindly, easy-mannered, dignified, self-possessed old gentleman." But during the party's long visit on a range of topics, Brother Brigham irritated Mark Twain by completely ignoring him. When the meeting ended, Twain said, "he put his hand on my head, beamed down at me in an admiring way, and said to my brother, 'Ah—your child, I presume? Boy or girl?'"

WHEN HOWARD W. HUNTER was a member of the Quorum of the Twelve, his trip to a stake conference in Mississippi caused considerable excitement among the members there. One boy in a local branch was thrilled to hear that Apostle Hunter was to be their conference visitor, and he wasted no time sharing the news with one of his young friends. "Guess who's coming to our next stake conference?" gushed the boy. "A possum hunter!"

· APRIL 11 ·

W EBSTER'S DICTIONARY DEFINES *responsibility* as being accountable for your behavior or actions.

As an example of the complete antithesis of responsibility, take the story that ran early in 1996 in a Wisconsin newspaper. Police picked up a twenty-two-year-old man for failure to carry his driver's license. The encounter ended with a search that uncovered cocaine concealed in the man's underwear.

The man's response? He declared his innocence, the newspaper said, "by saying the undershorts he was wearing were not his."

WHEN J. GOLDEN KIMBALL was on a mission in the southern United States, two of his colleagues were arrested and jailed in Tennessee. Throngs of people crowded around the jail, anxious to see them—and the elders responded by preaching and singing hymns through the prison bars with compelling fervor.

They witnessed so effectively that J. Golden said, "I am almost inclined to advocate putting our elders in jail once in a while, when they are unable to get a hearing in any other way."

WHEN THE GOING GETS TOUGH, so what? is the message of a story that's told of venerable Harvard Dean LeBaron Russell Briggs. A young student approached Dean Briggs one day and explained he hadn't completed his assignment because he wasn't feeling well. Looking the student piercingly in the eye, Dean Briggs said, "Mr. Smith, I think in time you may perhaps find that most of the work in the world is done by people who aren't feeling very well."

Early in 1974 during Spencer W. Kimball's first months as president of the Church, the pressures of his new calling were exhausting. The demands of his schedule—and the gravity of the many decisions he faced—weighed heavily upon him; fatigue and stress were his constant companions.

And so were perseverance and humor. "If I had known it was going to be like this," he quipped to his family, "I would never have run for the office."

YOU MAY HAVE HEARD the story of a Carthusian monk who described for a visitor how his order differed from others. "When it comes to good works, we don't match the Benedictines," said the monk. "As to preaching, we are not in a class with the Dominicans, and the Jesuits are away ahead of us in learning. But in the matter of humility, we're tops!"

· APRIL 16 ·

DURING AN AIRPLANE FLIGHT when he was
an apostle, Spencer W. Kimball was offered
coffee, tea, or Coca-Cola. "Do you have any
lemonade?" he asked. "No," said the flight
attendant, "but I could squeeze you some."
Elder Kimball feigned horror, declaring,
"Don't you squeeze me!"

OUR NEED TO DRAW CLOSE to spiritual influences is illustrated in a story told by Ardeth G. Kapp, former general president of the Young Women.

An eight-year-old boy who met Sister Kapp was thrilled to shake the hand of someone who had shaken hands with the prophet. "I'll never wash my hand," the boy said. She advised him to reconsider. "Okay," he said. "I'll wash my hand, but I'll save the water." He left the room and soon returned with a plastic bag full of the water he had used to wash. In a few minutes, he left again, then returned without the water—but with a wet T-shirt.

He'd found a better solution. "I drank the water," he said.

N. ELDON TANNER AND HIS FAMILY were never ashamed of the gospel of Christ. Once, a minister in Edmonton, Canada, asked N. Eldon's very young daughter, Helen, where she got her pretty brown eyes.

"From Heavenly Father," she said.

Helen's response ended up as the basis of the man's next sermon.

BRETHREN IN THE CHURCH shouldn't follow the example of the man who had season tickets to the basketball games at the university near his home.

During one basketball season, the man's wife died, but when the next game rolled around just a few days later, the man was there, as usual, even though the seat next to him, where his wife usually sat, was empty. "Couldn't you find a member of the family to come and sit in your wife's seat?" asked an acquaintance.

"No," said the sports fan. "They couldn't come. They've all gone to her funeral."

AUTHOR RICHARD EYRE ADVOCATES a number of creative ideas to help parents maintain the lines of communication with their children. But they don't always work, he said. Brother Eyre chose one late night to inquire how one of his sons was doing. They talked a little, then Brother Eyre lay down to listen as the boy described his day. Big mistake. "The next thing I knew," Brother Eyre said, "it was morning and my son was waking me up."

FOUR RELIGIOUS MYTHS:

- It's easy to get credit for doing good, but hard to get cash.
- Noah's wife was Joan of Ark.
- The fifth commandment is "Humor thy father and mother."
- It's hard to hear anything in church because the agnostics are so terrible.

Dᴀᴠɪᴅ O. MᴄKᴀʏ—well into his presidency and well past the age when most men don't climb anywhere but out of bed—tripped on a set of stairs leading up to a platform in front of a group of people. The audience gasped, but President McKay was fine. "It's awful to grow old," he said when he reached the podium, "but I prefer it to the alternative."

Matthew Cowley was in Japan once with some mission leaders when one of the men determined that he was going to follow a Japanese custom and eat a dried silkworm. "I have watched him ever since—and it worked," said Elder Cowley some time later. "His hair is getting silkier all the time."

YOU'RE NEVER DEFEATED UNTIL you quit trying. "Give up" shouldn't be in your vocabulary.

Or should it? The story of two men in a fierce disagreement—an Englishman and an Irishman—may give you pause for thought. As their discussion crept closer and closer to a fistfight, they agreed that the loser of the argument would be the man who first said the word *surrender*. The fight began. They traded devastating, angry blows. The Englishman went down, then staggered to his knees and stood up again. The Irishman was knocked down, but regained his feet and continued pounding on his opponent. Finally a punishing blow was landed; the Englishman dropped to the ground, and with the last of his energy, whispered, "Surrender."

"Thank goodness," gasped the Irishman. "I've been trying to remember that word for the last five minutes."

WHEN HEBER J. GRANT WAS YOUNG, he took singing lessons from a number of people—including his mother—but all his teachers eventually quit in despair. Heber persisted, though, and when he was about twenty-five, he asked a college professor to assess his abilities.

"He informed me that I could sing," said the future prophet, "but added, 'I would like to be at least forty miles away while you are doing it.'"

Gᴏᴅ ᴅᴏᴇs ɴᴏᴛɪᴄᴇ ᴜs, and he watches over us. But it is usually through another person that he meets our needs," said Spencer W. Kimball.

Dwan J. Young, former general Primary president, illustrated the principle with the story of three young boys who got their kite stuck in a tree. They tried a number of different ways of getting it down, but none were successful. Finally they decided to pray. As they opened their eyes at the end of their prayer, a car came toward them. The woman driving noticed their woeful faces and stopped to ask if they needed any help. After they explained their plight, she pulled her car right under the limb where the kite was stuck, climbed up on top her car's roof, and then, with a long stick, reached the kite and pulled it down.

When one of the boys got home, he told his mother what had happened. "Who helped you get your kite down?" asked his mom.

"Heavenly Father," said the boy.

ONE DAY WHEN THE PROPHET JOSEPH was at his parents' home, a party of armed militia stormed in and declared to Lucy Mack Smith that they had come to kill her son. Joseph listened to the men make their threats, then greeted each one with a smile and a handshake. "They stared at him as if he were a spectre," Sister Smith said. The Prophet then sat down with the men and shared his feelings about the Church and about the persecution the Church members had suffered. After talking with them some time in this way, he said, "Mother, I believe I will go home now—Emma will be expecting me."

"At this, two of the men sprang to their feet and declared that he should not go alone, as it would be unsafe—that they would go with him, in order to protect him," Sister Smith said. "Accordingly, the three left together."

WHEN THE RELIEF SOCIETY BUILDING was being built across the street from the Salt Lake Temple, Relief Society sisters everywhere were invited to contribute five dollars toward its construction. One sister remembers thinking how much money that was at the time—and how she wanted to spend it on something for her young children instead. Her mother prodded her to pitch in, though. "Just give your five dollars, Barbara," said her mother. "You'll always be glad you did."

Many years later, that young woman walked into the Relief Society Building almost every week. "And whenever I did, I was glad I gave my five dollars," said Barbara B. Smith, who became general president of the Relief Society.

Is it hard for you to forgive those who wrong you? Remember the example of Jens Christian Johansen, a Danish convert who came to Utah around 1860. In his journal one day he wrote, "As I piled my hay and did my work, I took twelve piles and stuck them over the fence to my neighbor, as they had no hay for the horses and cows; and we could see a little gone from our area the night before.

"I would rather give them a little," he wrote, "than have them steal."

ON HIS WAY HOME TO UTAH after a mission in Hawaii, Joseph F. Smith encountered a drunken band of ruffians who were threatening to kill any Mormons they found. The leader of the gang pointed two pistols at Elder Smith, cursed, and asked angrily, "Are you a Mormon?"

"Yesiree," Elder Smith boldly replied. "Dyed in the wool, true blue, through and through." The outlaw was dumbfounded. "Well," he said, "you are the blankedty-blankedest pleasantest man I ever met! Shake hands, young fellow. I am glad to see a man that stands up for his convictions."

On a tour of the Church's woolen mills, J. Golden Kimball had his long coat snagged in the whirring machinery, which spun him around several times, then threw him to the floor.

The young tour guide was aghast as the Church leader lay there silently. "Brother Kimball," he said, "speak to me! Speak to me!"

J. Golden, obviously, wasn't hurt. "I don't know why I should," he said. "I passed you twelve times just now, and not once did you speak to me!"

DAVID LAWRENCE MCKAY, father of David O. McKay, was thirty-seven years old with three children, a pregnant wife, and a farm to run when he received a mission call to Scotland. His wife, Jennette Evans McKay, immediately supported the call, but David, mindful of his many obligations, was torn with indecision.

As he expressed his concerns to family members about the timing of the call, his uncle urged him to consider another factor: his wife's strong will. "You may be right and you may be wrong," the uncle said, "but if Jennette has set her mind that you should answer the mission call, you might as well give in!"

AMAN ONCE ASKED J. Golden Kimball if he believed Jonah was really swallowed by a whale. "When I get to heaven I'll ask Jonah," said the Church leader.

"What if he is not there?" asked the cynic.

"Then you will have to ask him," said J. Golden.

LOOKING FOR A GOOD parenting tip? Former general Primary president Michaelene P. Grassli quoted Dr. Lynn Scoresby: "When we make mistakes, the Savior doesn't say, 'Go to your room.' He says, 'Come unto me.'"

J. GOLDEN KIMBALL LED SOME foreign leaders on a tour of Salt Lake City, but at every stop one of the guests dismissed the beauties of the city with tales of the greater glory of his own homeland. Seeing a great building, he remarked that his people could have built it in half the time. The tour continued on that note—as J. Golden grew increasingly irritated—until the group passed the Salt Lake Temple. "What is that building there?" asked the arrogant visitor.

"——ed if I know," said J. Golden. "It wasn't there yesterday."

SETTING PRIORITIES IS OFTEN THE KEY to accomplishment and success.

A story, attributed to the former head of the Royal Canadian Mounted Police, describes an essay question that was part of a quiz for young applicants who were trying to get into the Mounties.

"You're at the scene of an explosion," reads the quiz. "There are numerous casualties. You also notice a drunk driver who you recognize as a prominent local government leader. A woman on the scene starts to give birth. Someone is drowning in a nearby canal, while a fight breaks out which could result in damage and even loss of life. In a few words, describe what you would do."

One applicant's response: "I would remove my uniform and mingle with the crowd."

"TEMPTATION IS LIKE A TIGER chained to a pole," said author J. Randolph Ayre: It's only dangerous if you step within its reach.

Brother Ayre told a story to illustrate that precept. After World War II, an American military officer was charged to establish order and remove the criminal elements from a large city in the Pacific islands. Soon after starting his work, a man approached the officer with a $10,000 bribe, which the officer could have if he'd look the other way while a gambling dive was set up. The officer said no. The next day, the gambler returned and offered $25,000, but the officer stood firm; he had the man thrown out of his office. Soon the gambler returned a third time, this time with $50,000. Again the officer threw the gambler out, then went to his commanding officer and asked for a transfer.

"What's the matter?" asked the man's superior. "Is that man making it too hot for you?"

"No," said the officer. "He's getting too near my price."

Dᴜʀɪɴɢ ʜɪs ᴍɪssɪᴏɴ ɪɴ ᴛʜᴇ southern states, J. Golden Kimball was afflicted with a severe case of malaria. He was walking in Chattanooga, Tennessee—"as yellow as a parchment," he said—when he happened upon a physician who warned him that if he didn't seek treatment, he would die.

"I will not," said J. Golden. "I'm a Mormon: You can't kill them."

INSTEAD OF FOCUSING ON THE emotional or physical costs of your hardships, think about what they're giving you.

One Sunday, an aged Saint who had crossed the plains with the ill-fated Martin Handcart Company listened to a teacher bemoan the great hardships suffered by its participants. Finally, the old man stood to speak.

"I have pulled my handcart when I was so weak and weary from illness and lack of food that I could hardly put one foot ahead of the other. I have looked ahead to a certain point and said, 'I can go only that far and there I must give up.' When I reached that point, the cart began pushing me. I have looked back to see who was pushing my cart, but saw no one. I knew then that the angels of God were there.

"Was I sorry I chose to come by handcart? No. Neither then nor any minute of my life since then. The price we paid to become acquainted with God was a privilege to pay."

THE ONLY WHIPPING Joseph Fielding Smith ever received was when his father, Joseph F. Smith, thought he had told a lie—when the young man actually had not. Years later, the future prophet reminded the current prophet of the experience, complete with the fact that he was innocent of what he'd been punished for.

"Oh, well," said the senior Smith, "We'll let that apply on something you did when you didn't get caught."

WHEN SPENCER W. KIMBALL was president of the Church and Spencer Kinard was the voice of *Music and the Spoken Word,* the two were on an elevator when a third man, an acquaintance of Brother Kinard, stepped on with them. "Push three for me, will you, Spence?" he said.

"Surely," said President Kimball, who pushed the button.

AFTER SPENDING MANY YEARS in New Zealand, Matthew Cowley gained a great appreciation for Maori and Polynesian customs. One such custom: rubbing noses. "We don't really rub," he explained. "You just press your forehead and your nose against the nose and forehead of the other person.

"It's a wonderful thing," he said. "You can always tell who's keeping the Word of Wisdom down there."

HEBER J. GRANT WAS IN A MEETING in which his bishop expressed a need for financial support. Heber, despite his young age, had fifty dollars in his pocket, and after the meeting he gave it to the bishop. But the bishop, not wanting to cause a hardship on Heber and his family, took just five dollars and handed the rest back. "Bishop Wooley," said Heber, "by what right do you rob me of putting the Lord in my debt? Didn't you preach here today that the Lord rewards fourfold? My mother is a widow and she needs two hundred dollars."

"My boy," asked the bishop, "do you believe that if I take this other forty-five dollars, you will get your two hundred quicker?"

"Certainly," said Heber.

On the way home from the meeting, Heber got an idea, and when he acted on it, he made $218.50.

"Someone will say it would have happened anyway," he said many years later. "I do not think it would have."

DURING HIS TRAVELS as an apostle, Spencer W. Kimball tried to avoid the indulgences his hosts often wanted to provide him. Once a benefactor insisted on shining Elder Kimball's shoes, which the apostle submitted to with some reluctance. "There," said the man when the shoes were polished. "Finished!"

"Oh no! Not yet!" replied the apostle, reaching for the man's brush and shoe creme. "You sit here," he said, "and I'll shine yours."

A POEM QUOTED BY AUTHOR Alma Heaton probably contains some good advice for young men and young women:

> Before I heard the doctors tell
> The danger of a kiss,
> I had considered kissing you
> The nearest thing to bliss
>
> But now I know biology
> I sit and sigh and moan,
> Six million mad bacteria
> And I thought we were alone.

A YOUNG, REBELLIOUS MAN once sat in Spencer W. Kimball's office, and in response to President Kimball's comments about his actions, said, "These are your own opinions."

The prophet's response is worth remembering. "If that were true," he said, "I would agree with you. But you have forgotten one thing . . .

"Your logic is hardly equal to the inspiration and revelation from the Lord that I am representing to you. God said the act is sin. Numerous prophets claim the act is sin. The act is sin.

"Yes, my friend, if it were your mind against mine, your logic against mine, your perception against my limited ability, then I would retire and leave you to your deliberations. But I am expressing not my own opinion but the word of the Lord of heaven, and I am telling you God's truth. To compare your opinion with the Lord's proven truth might be like a grain of sand compared to the bulk of Mt. Everest."

GROWING UP IN CANADA, Ardeth G. Kapp spent many hours working in the fields on her family's farm, often working with her unschooled but very wise father. The lessons she learned covered more than agriculture.

"We'd put up a fence together," she recalled, "and he'd say, 'Keep your eye on the horizon and you'll keep the posts in line. It's the direction that's important, and the purpose, not the distance.'"

Or, as Sister Kapp and her father were irrigating the fields, he'd show his daughter how to jump a ditch. "He'd say, 'There are a lot of ditches in life, and many you'll have to cross alone. Keep your eye on the other side and give it all you've got, and you'll make it.'"

Some find budgeting extremely painful," said Marvin J. Ashton in 1981. "But I promise you, it is never fatal."

Camilla Eyring Kimball learned that lesson. Well before she married Spencer W. Kimball, she lived in Provo, Utah, with her uncle and his wife while all three of them attended BYU. Camilla studied home economics, in preparation for a teaching career—and she and her uncle and aunt were experts in keeping their home economical. Her years at BYU were difficult and poverty-ridden, she said.

"One time I received a telegram from my father asking why I had not written home," Sister Kimball recalled. "The reason was that I did not have two cents for a stamp."

THE EXAMPLE OF A SCOUTMASTER, Ray Ertmann, who was always, always, available to his Scouts is recounted by Chieko N. Okazaki, first counselor in the general Relief Society presidency. "His house was always open to us," recalled one of his young charges many years later. "He said, 'As long as the front porch light is on, you can come in and see me.'"

Sister Okazaki added a point that must have pleased the power company: "And Brother Ertmann left the porch light on all night, every night."

Elder ElRay Christiansen told the story of an inactive brother who had a consistent answer for all the Church leaders who called on him. "I will come to church when I get straightened out," he always said.

"I was called on to speak at that man's funeral," said the man's elders quorum president. "He was in church, all right, and he was surely straightened out."

· MAY 21 ·

BEFORE RUTH H. FUNK BECAME general president of the Young Women, she was attending a Church committee meeting and was asked without prior notice to play the piano during the opening song.

Sister Funk, who had forgotten her glasses, walked to the front of the room. Her friend—and later, her counselor—Hortense Child was sitting in an aisle seat, and as Sister Funk walked past she plucked Sister Child's glasses right off her nose, put them on, and didn't miss a note in the song.

She knew, as Proverbs says, that where there is no vision, the people perish.

Faith often precedes knowledge, Alma teaches. Case in point: A lesson Hugh B. Brown learned from his older brother, Bud, when they were young. They were up in the top of their father's barn, where Bud was helping Hugh swing from the rafters. "I will swing you back and forth," Bud said. "When you get going pretty good, I will tell you when to let loose of that rafter and when to grab the next one." Hugh swung. Bud said, "Now." Hugh had faith. "I let loose of the rafter," he said, "but the other one was not within reach."

The knowledge Hugh gained: Be careful where you invest your faith. "It took me six hours to wake up," he said.

Eating wasn't a high priority to Howard W. Hunter. His two daughters-in-law once described a cross-country trip their families took with Elder and Sister Hunter—which included stops at many important Church history sites but not many stops at roadside cafés. "Dad would never stop to eat," they told the *Church News*. Each morning as they climbed into their car, they'd plan to stop for breakfast or lunch but usually ended up driving until dinnertime.

"Hunger," they said, "was a memorable part of that trip."

Rise to meet your challenges, said Elaine Cannon, former president of the Young Women. Your attitude determines your altitude.

She illustrated with a story about a young girl who poured out some of her miseries to—of all people—her brother. "It just isn't fair," said the girl. "You got the curly hair and the straight nose."

The brother—"brothers are so wonderful," said Sister Cannon—answered, "Well, you got the curly nose and the straight hair!"

THE JOY OF TEACHING, said Ardeth G. Kapp, lies in unlocking doors. She recounts the story of one young boy who struggled with long division. "For Jeff," she said, "there were hours and hours of constant encouragement by his teacher while he tried to understand for himself the difficult process of long division."

A week of struggle and effort passed. "On Friday, in the late afternoon," said Sister Kapp, "while his classmates were quietly reading their favorite books, Jeff finally released from his worn-down pencil onto his very smudgy paper some numbers that for the first time, for him, made sense.

"In an explosion of ecstasy he burst forth with words never before spoken by this timid yet persistent child. 'Hey,' he said out loud, 'I'm not dumb after all!'

"For the teacher," said Sister Kapp, "it was like beautiful, colorful fireworks bursting forth in a darkened sky."

J. GOLDEN KIMBALL AND Francis M. Lyman encouraged the Saints to subscribe to the *Improvement Era* magazine during a conference in Panaca, Nevada. After a long day of meetings—on a fast day—Elder Lyman introduced J. Golden around 4:00 P.M. "Now, Brother Kimball, get up and tell them about the *Improvement Era*," said the apostle.

J. Golden complied. He said, "All you men that will take the *Era* if we will let you go home now, raise your right hand."

His short sermon worked. "There was not a single man who did not raise his hand and subscribe and pay two dollars cash then and there for the *Era*," J. Golden said.

LaVELL EDWARDS, BYU's football coach, loves Cougars, and vice versa, but doesn't quite trust most other animals, including Rams, Nittany Lions, Wildcats, Bulldogs, Huskies . . . and housecats. Part of his suspicion may stem from the winter night when his daughter, Ann, brought home two strays and begged to keep them. "Are they males?" asked the coach. "Sure," said his daughter. "Their names are Sam and George."

"That spring," said Ann, "Sam and George had thirteen kittens between them."

BACK WHEN PEOPLE AROUND the world were perplexed by polygamy, George Q. Cannon, who had five wives and thirty-five children, sometimes contributed to the confusion. On a mission in London, Elder Cannon ordered three top-grade razors for three of his sons, who were soon to turn twenty-one. "Triplets?" asked the shopkeeper. "Why, no, indeed," said Elder Cannon. "They were born several days apart throughout the month."

SOMETIME IN ETERNITIES TO COME," said Delbert L. Stapley, "we will see that our trials were calculated to cause us to turn to our Heavenly Father for strength and support. Any affliction or suffering we are called upon to bear may be directed to give us experience, refinement, and perfection."

Marvin J. Ashton illustrated that principle with the story of a young man who was concerned about the trials facing his mother. "If God is omnipotent and knows all, why does he put my mother through the agony of continual sufferings when he already knows what the outcome will be?" asked the young man.

Elder Ashton's response: "Your mother's trials are not tests so the Lord can measure her. They are tests and trials so that your mother can measure herself. It is most important that she know her strengths in adversity and grow from the experiences."

JOHN TAYLOR AND JOSEPH F. SMITH were both present the day Heber J. Grant, who was then just twenty-four, was named president of the Tooele Stake. After Heber failed to bear his testimony during the meeting when he was sustained, President Taylor asked the young man if he knew the Church was true. Young Heber said he didn't. Elder Smith immediately called for the young man's release. "I am not going to complain," replied Heber.

President Taylor greatly enjoyed Heber's response—and he ended the discussion with a comment that's often applicable today. "Joseph, Joseph, Joseph," said the prophet, "he knows it just as well as you do. The only thing he does not know is that he does know it."

HEBER J. GRANT SAID, "We should have an ambition, we should have a desire, to work to the full extent of our ability."

Sometimes we should also have earplugs. President Grant practiced his singing one day next to a dentist's office. "The people in the hall," he said, "decided that someone was having his teeth extracted."

CHIEKO N. OKAZAKI REMEMBERS an autumn Sunday not too many months before her husband, Ed, passed away. Ed had bought two crates of oranges the day before, and the Okazakis drove to a park in downtown Salt Lake City to give one crate away to the homeless people who gathered there.

When the Okazakis left the park, they walked past a homeless brother who shivered in a T-shirt in the autumn cold. "When I glanced back over my shoulder, there was my wonderful husband slipping off his jacket and helping this man into it," said Sister Okazaki. "He just said quietly, 'You need this more than I do.'

"And then, in his shirt sleeves, he came walking toward me with the biggest smile on his face," she said.

"Nothing in the world—and I mean nothing—made Ed as happy as helping someone else."

SPENCER W. KIMBALL TOLD THE STORY of a young Mormon soldier in World War II who wore both a standard wristwatch and an older, larger pocket watch. His buddies noticed him regularly looking at both watches, and asked why he checked the time twice.

"The wristwatch tells me the time here where we are, but the big watch Pa gave me tells me the time it is in Utah," said the soldier. "When the big watch says 5:00 A.M., I know dad is rolling out to milk the cows. And any night when it says 7:30, I know the whole family is around a well-spread table on their knees thanking the Lord for what's on the table and asking him to watch over me and keep me clean and honorable.

"It's those things that make me want to fight when the going gets tough," said the young man. "I can find out what time it is here easy enough. What I want to know is what time it is in Utah."

IN THE MEDICAL PROFESSION, there are house calls—and then there was Ellis Reynolds Shipp, an early Latter-day Saint who was one of the first women physicians in Utah. She had six children before she earned her medical degree in New Jersey in 1878, and during her medical practice she delivered more than 5,000 babies.

Her fee for prenatal and obstetrical care was twenty-five dollars, which was often paid in chickens, butter, and eggs. Her fee also covered ten postnatal visits, during which Dr. Shipp would—compare this to any doctor you know who still makes house calls—monitor her patients' conditions, change their beds, and cook them a meal.

GREAT PHYSICAL INFIRMITIES never dimmed Howard W. Hunter's sparkling wit. During his short term as president of the Church, he spoke at a sacrament meeting in his home ward. One of the prophet's close friends and longtime neighbors, Jon M. Huntsman, and another man helped the prophet return to his seat after he had delivered his sermon.

The prophet whispered to Brother Huntsman, "Just drop me anywhere!"

JUST WHEN YOU THINK you've escaped pride . . .

A Sunday School teacher gave a lesson about the arrogant Pharisee who prayed in the temple next to the humble publican and expressed thanks to the Lord that he wasn't like his prayer-mate. The publican, meanwhile, bowed his head and smote his breast and asked the Lord to forgive him for his sins.

The Sunday School teacher's suggestion? The members of the class should all thank God they were not like that Pharisee!

ONE SUNDAY AT A LONELY country church, only one worshiper showed up for Sunday morning services. The pastor asked the man, a local farmer, if they shouldn't just cancel the service, but the farmer said, "Pastor, if I drove my hay wagon out in the field to feed the cows, and only one cow showed up, I wouldn't deny that cow her dinner."

So the preacher delivered his sermon. He preached and preached; he pounded the pulpit; he harangued against evil for a full two hours. At the end of his sermon he shook hands with the lone member of his congregation and asked how he liked the service.

"Well, pastor," said the farmer, "if I drove my hay wagon out to the field and only one cow came up to eat, I wouldn't deny the one cow, but I wouldn't give it the whole load, either."

PLAN AHEAD. Be prepared. Cover your bases. Be like the boy who came home with a terrible report card. When he gave it to his dad, his dad said he'd never seen a worse report card.

"Yes, dad," said the boy. "What do you think the problem is? Heredity or environment?"

HUSBANDS, NO MATTER HOW LONG you've been married, are you still actively courting your wife? Take a tip from Gordon B. Hinckley's father, Bryant S. Hinckley, who told a story about a sleeping farmer and his wife whose house was swept up one dark night by a cyclone. The storm dropped them, bed and all, in the middle of an alfalfa field some distance from their disheveled house, and despite their safe landing, the farmer's wife cried inconsolably.

The farmer tried to comfort her by assuring her that the storm was past and they were safe, but she continued to cry. "Think of it, Henry," she wailed. "This is the first time in twenty years we have been out together!"

Sᴘᴇᴀᴋɪɴɢ ᴏɴ ᴘʀɪᴏʀɪᴛɪᴇs ɪɴ 1974, Harold B. Lee said, "Most men forget that the first priority should be to maintain their own spiritual and physical strength, then comes their family, then the church, and then their professions."

Get those mixed up, and you risk becoming like the accountant who had a heart attack and died right at his desk. Actually he didn't die right away, he just collapsed and suffered for a little while, but by the time he got three bids from the paramedics, he was gone.

When Hugh B. Brown was a stake president in western Canada in the 1920s, he learned, he said, that tolerance was "understanding, and seeing beyond the smoke of a cigarette and into the soul of a man." On a trip to find a new bishop for a struggling ward, he and his two counselors once ran across a Church member driving toward them down a road, smoking a cigar. They stopped to talk. "I said, 'Burt, we want you to be the bishop of the Tabor Ward,'" said Elder Brown.

The man held up his cigar. "H—," he said. "With this?"

"H—, no," answered the young stake president. "Without it."

"By h—," said the man, "I'll try it."

"He never smoked again," said Elder Brown, "and became one of the best bishops we had."

MATTHEW COWLEY PICKED UP a Primary teacher's training manual one day and leafed through its chapters. One heading was "A child needs love." Another was "A child needs recognition." Another: "A child needs discipline."

"And I said, 'Why limit it to the child?'" said Brother Cowley.

ALWAYS CULTIVATE A SPIRIT of gratitude," said Lorenzo Snow.

Take a lesson from a self-possessed old grandmother who took her grandson to the beach. For a brief moment, she turned away, and her grandson was caught in the undertow and swept out to sea. Both the Coast Guard and a police helicopter were summoned as a lifeguard valiantly rowed after the boy. Eventually, after great effort, he was retrieved and brought to shore, where the lifeguard resuscitated the boy until his breathing was restored.

"Excuse me," the grandmother said. "He had a hat . . ."

WHEN WAS THE LAST TIME you feasted on the word?" asked Bonnie D. Parkin, second counselor in the Young Women's general presidency in a Young Women's satellite broadcast. "Did you know feasting could be so guilt-free?"

Sister Parkin joked that she can gain weight just by looking at a menu—but then said that's not a problem when we're feasting on the word of God. "Did you know the Lord doesn't expect us to diet?" Sister Parkin asked. She quoted the last line of 2 Nephi 9:51: "Let your soul delight in fatness."

When Hugh B. Brown was called to preside over the British Mission, he leased his large home in California to a successful businessman. But soon after the Browns arrived in England, they were informed that the man's lease was broken: He had killed his wife and her lover as they sat on a piano bench in the Brown's living room, and he was going to prison.

"There was only one thing to do," said Elder Brown, "and that was to carry on with chin up and try to keep a sense of humor.

"If this jealous husband had wanted to kill his wife," he said, "you would think he might have taken her outside instead of mussing up our front room, but we do not all do things the same way."

WHEN J. GOLDEN KIMBALL was president
of the Southern States Mission, he approached
the leaders of a local town about using their
courthouse to hold a mission conference. It
was the kind of assignment from which some
missionaries returned covered with tar and
feathers—if they returned at all.

J. Golden told the elders who were with
him to hold back and let him do the talking.
"If they kill me," he said, "you need not
bother further."

CHIEKO N. OKAZAKI TELLS THE STORY of a reporter for Utah's *Deseret News*, who came upon a down-on-his-luck traveler at a freeway rest stop one hot summer day in the desert west of Salt Lake City. The man asked for gas money from his fellow travelers, and they responded with donated gasoline, ice chips, and—from an older man in a beat-up car—cash.

"As we walked back to our cars, I asked the elderly man if he ever worried about being 'taken,'" wrote the reporter.

"Nope," said the man. "I just bought myself a good feeling. Cheap. If he's taking advantage of me, that's his problem, not mine."

AS A YOUNG BOY GROWING UP in Idaho, Howard W. Hunter made money by selling papers, framing pictures, and fixing alarm clocks. Another job was sorting lemons, removing the green ones from the yellow ones. "This was one of the few tasks for which he had no aptitude whatever," wrote a biographer, for President Hunter was colorblind.

DURING ONE OF MATTHEW COWLEY'S missions to New Zealand, a father asked Elder Cowley to give his baby a name and a blessing. Brother Cowley agreed. As they were about to begin, the father added, "By the way, give him his vision when you give him a name. He was born blind."

Elder Cowley was unnerved, but he thought, *Why not?* "I had faith in that father's faith," he said, and he pronounced the blessing. Several years later he saw the child again; the boy's vision was perfectly normal. "'Lay your hands upon the sick, and they shall recover,'" said Elder Cowley, quoting the Doctrine and Covenants. "There is no question about it in my mind."

VON PACKARD, A PROMINENT DENTIST from Carlsbad, California, and a former mission president, summarized what happened in the Garden of Eden with brevity and levity.

"Adam blamed Eve, and Eve blamed the snake, and the snake didn't have a leg to stand on."

SHORTLY BEFORE HIS SAN FRANCISCO 49ers won the 1995 Super Bowl, the heralded Mormon quarterback Steve Young remembered his early days in football when he arrived at BYU in 1980. "I really didn't know how to throw back then," he said. "I learned to throw at Brigham Young, mostly from Jim McMahon. We were about the same size and had the same athletic abilities. It was really good for me, because he had no bad habits."

Jim McMahon, noted nonconformist—no bad habits? Young pondered some of the exploits attributed to his maverick predecessor at BYU, then reconsidered. "I mean, naked golf, that's different," he said.

MARY ELIZABETH ROLLINS LIGHTNER, one of the Church's earliest converts, had a burning desire to read the Book of Mormon, but a serious shortage of copies made it almost impossible. The one copy in Kirtland, Ohio, in 1830, belonged to Isaac Morley, president of Kirtland's small gathering of Saints.

Mary went to see Brother Morley one evening and asked if she could borrow the book. He agreed only on the condition that she return it before breakfast the following morning; he had barely had time to read a chapter in it himself. Mary dashed home with the treasure and read far into the night.

Before breakfast the next morning she showed Brother Morley how much she had read. He was doubtful. "I don't believe you can tell me one word of it," he said. Mary said: "I then repeated the first verse, and also the outlines of the history of Nephi. He gazed at me in surprise and said, 'Child, take this book home and finish it; I can wait.'"

EVER WONDER IF THE LORD watches out for his people? Mary Elizabeth Rollins Lightner was one of a group of early Saints in Ohio that was pushed westward by mob persecution. Mary's party packed all they owned and fled toward the Missouri River, but found they didn't have enough money to hire a ferry to carry them across. The enterprising Saints set out fishing lines in the hope of catching enough fish to trade for a ride across the river, but in the morning their catch was largely disappointing: only three small fish and one fourteen-pound catfish.

One of the brethren in the party cut open the catfish to clean it and found three shiny silver half-dollars—exactly the sum needed to ferry the Saints across the river.

"This was considered a miracle," wrote Mary, "and caused great rejoicing among us."

DAVID O. McKAY WAS DELIGHTED one day when a policeman pulled him over for speeding. The experience countered an impression held by some people, said the aged prophet, that he was slowing down in his old age.

· JUNE 24 ·

THE APOSTLE MARK SAYS to take no thought beforehand, neither premeditate, what you should speak when you're called upon. On the other hand . . .

A man who was asked to speak at a neighboring church took his small boy with him to fulfill the assignment. As they walked into the chapel, the man noticed a collection box on a table in the foyer of the church. He took a quarter from his pocket and dropped it into the box.

After the sermon, the pastor of the church walked back into the foyer with the man and his boy and picked up the collection box. "We have a tradition here to give the proceeds of our weekly collection to whoever comes to speak to us," he said, and he tipped the box into the speaker's hand. Out rolled the quarter.

On the way home, the boy said to his father, "You should have put more into it, and you would have got more out of it."

GEORGE A. SMITH, GRANDFATHER to President George Albert Smith, was called "elder" and "president" by the early Saints. He was an apostle for thirty-nine years and spent eight years as first counselor to Brigham Young. But he was best known among Utah's Indians for his wig, eyeglasses, and false teeth, which he sometimes removed in their presence. The Indians called him "Non-choko-wicher," which means "Man-who-takes-himself-apart."

JANET G. LEE, THE WIFE of former BYU president Rex E. Lee, remembered when their daughter, Stephanie, was registering for kindergarten. As part of a test to judge the girl's skill level, a teacher handed Stephanie a box of crayons and instructed her to write her name in her favorite color. But Stephanie—who could write not only her own name but also the names of everyone in her family—did nothing. Twice more the teacher asked Stephanie to write her name, but each time Stephanie failed to respond.

On the way home, Sister Lee asked her daughter what the problem was. "The teacher said to choose my favorite color," the girl replied, "and there wasn't a pink crayon in the box!"

An EXPERIENCE AT ONE WARD'S Mutual swimming party illustrates the difference between faith and works.

During the opening prayer, a counselor in the bishopric heard splashing. He opened one eye and saw that a young boy who didn't know how to swim had fallen into the deep end of the pool. "His eyes reflected fear and terror," said the brother, who had not planned to swim himself. "I took two steps, dove into the pool—suit, shoes, and all—pulled the young man to the side and helped him out." The boy sat on the lip of the pool; the counselor stood in the water while the prayer, despite what had just happened, went on and on.

"I think the young man would have drowned if we had waited for the prayer to end," said the counselor. Then he added, "I think we have to keep an eye open and be ready to do whatever is necessary to save our youth."

Boyd Jarman—a member of the BYU basketball team that won the National Invitational tournament in 1951—was awestruck when he stepped into New York City's Madison Square Garden for the first time.

Boyd, who had grown up on a quiet ranch in Wyoming, checked out the massive, empty, echoing arena during the Cougars' first practice. "Boy," he said, "this barn sure will hold a lot of hay."

N. ELDON TANNER ONCE MET with a father who was worried about the choices his son was making. President Tanner asked the father if his family held regular family prayer. "Well, no, but sometimes," said the man. "You know, we are too busy and we go to work at different times, and therefore it is most difficult for our family to get together for family prayer."

President Tanner asked, "If you knew that your boy was sick nigh unto death, would you be able to get your family together each night and morning for a week to pray that his life might be spared?"

"Why, of course," said the father.

"There are other ways of losing a boy than by death," said President Tanner.

"Where families pray together," he said, "they usually stay together, and their ideals are higher, they feel more secure, and they have a greater love for one another."

IT'S NOT ENOUGH TO BE GOOD, said Henry David Thoreau; you've got to be good for something. Jacob de Jager illustrated the principle with the story of two men who were sailing a hot-air balloon over Holland. After they'd been blown far off their course, they dropped their balloon low enough to see a lone man walking on a deserted road.

"Where are we?" they shouted.

The man looked up. "You are in a balloon!" he answered.

The two balloonists tried another tack to get clearer directions. They shouted to the man, "Where are you?"

"I am on the ground!" yelled the man.

"Perfectly true," said Brother de Jager, "but totally useless."

ElRay Christiansen told a story about a wealthy man in Denmark who joined the Church and, at the cost of almost all his belongings, made the commitment to come to Utah. He worked hard after settling with the Saints, and made another fortune—but in the process lost his testimony of the gospel.

One of his friends tried to help the man regain his eternal perspective. "Lars," said the friend, "it is not good to think only of money. You cannot take it with you, you know."

"Vell, den," said Lars, "I vill not go."

THE CHURCH IS TRUE, but that doesn't mean its officers don't sometimes misstep. One example: When the Church created its Public Affairs Department to handle media relations and other public communication functions, its original name was the Department of External Communications.

The problem was, the name was often shortened to "Ex. Communications"—which created exactly the wrong image for the new department.

WILFORD WOODRUFF FOUND that the Lord will provide . . . in the Lord's own way.

As a missionary in Missouri in 1830, he knocked at the door of a man who'd been active in persecuting the Saints. "In those days it was the custom of the Missourians to ask you to eat even though they were hostile to you, so he asked us to take breakfast," Elder Woodruff wrote. "He knew we were Mormons, and as soon as we began to eat, he began to swear about the Mormons. He had a large platter of bacon and eggs, and plenty of bread on the table, and his swearing did not hinder our eating, for the harder he swore the harder we ate." When they finished, the missionaries thanked their host and left.

"The last we heard he was still swearing," Elder Woodruff said. "I trust the Lord will reward him for the breakfast."

DURING A TRIP TO WASHINGTON, D.C., to dedicate the new Washington Temple, President Spencer W. Kimball was invited to offer the daily prayer at the start of a day's session of the United States Senate. But as the time for the prayer approached, only six senators were present in the Senate chamber.

"That's all right," said the prophet to one of his apologetic hosts. "I was not going to pray to them anyway."

AFTER CALLING A MAN TO SERVE as patriarch in a New York stake, Elder Harold B. Lee was asked to help set the man apart.

The man's wife was anxious about her husband's new responsibility to pronounce the lineage of the members of her stake. She thought: "He hasn't been a student of ancient languages—how is he going to know?"

As these thoughts ran through her mind, she saw Elder Lee place his hands on the man's head. "A light came from behind you and went right through you and into him," she told Elder Lee afterward. "I thought to myself, 'Isn't that a strange coincidence that the sunlight has come in just at this moment?'

"Then I realized that there was no sunlight," she said. "I was witnessing the answer to my question. . . . I knew where he was going to get that information: From the revelations of Almighty God."

MATTHEW COWLEY FILLED IN for President J. Reuben Clark at the dedication of a chapel in New York City. After the dedication he met with three New York ministers. One of the men had a question. "All right, what is it?" said Elder Cowley. "I always know the answers to all of these questions. My answer is generally, 'I don't know.'"

MARVIN J. ASHTON ONCE accompanied Spencer W. Kimball when the prophet visited the Utah state prison to meet with two inmates in the warden's office. One inmate was convicted of murder, the other of manslaughter. "What do you say?" wondered Elder Ashton. "What do you do? Do you say, 'Aren't you ashamed of yourselves? What a waste for you to be in such a place as this?'"

In the meeting, the two convicts looked down at the floor. President Kimball waited until one of them looked up, then caught his eye and said, "Tell me about your mother." The man talked; he poured out his soul; he cried. When he finished speaking, the prophet asked a similar question of the other young man, which produced a similar result.

"I learned more about interviewing in those fifteen minutes than in any similar period in my life," said Elder Ashton. "No condemnation. No judging. Only displaying a real interest in the person and his circumstances."

You've heard the advice: Be careful what you ask for; you might get it.

Two inebriated brothers learned that lesson near the Salt Lake Temple many years ago, said Marion G. Romney. Two Church security men were working up near the top of the temple one night when they saw the two drunks leaning on the gate near the temple's front doors. One of the men tilted his head up to look up at the golden statue on the temple's top spire. "Oh, Moroni, speak to me," he said.

One of the quick-witted Church security men answered, "Yes, what is it you want?"

CHEATERS ALWAYS LOSE IN THE END—and sometimes they lose right in the beginning. The story is told of a teacher who noticed that one of her students had copied the answers on a test from the boy who'd been sitting next to him. She called the father of the boy she suspected of cheating, but he didn't believe it; he wanted proof. So the teacher read the first question on the test: "Who was the sixteenth president of the United States?" Both boys had answered Abraham Lincoln. The next question was "Who was the seventeenth president?" Both boys had answered Lyndon Johnson.

The third question was the clincher, said the teacher. The question was "What were the causes of the Civil War?" "The fellow across the aisle wrote, 'I don't know,'" explained the teacher, "and your son wrote, 'Neither do I.'"

"THE OLDER WE GET and the longer we labor in the Church, the more there is that we can do," said George Q. Morris in a 1952 conference talk. "There is no need for any person in this church to have an empty hand or an empty heart."

Late in her life, Camilla Eyring Kimball had no empty hands despite the limits of advancing age. "A few months ago I took up painting," she said after she entered her ninth decade. "When someone asked why, I had to say, 'What else can you take up at ninety-two?'"

WHEN THE SAINTS WERE being driven out of Missouri, young Eliza R. Snow—who later would become the second president of the Relief Society—was confronted by a member of the Missouri militia. She was walking west in the snow, away from her home, on a bitterly cold day. The solder said to the girl, "Well, I think this will cure you of your faith!"

"No, sir," responded Eliza, "It will take more than this to cure me of my faith." The man dropped his eyes. "I must confess," he said, "you are a better soldier than I am."

"I passed on," wrote Sister Snow years later, "thinking that, unless he was above the average of his fellows in that section, I was not highly complimented by his confession."

IN YOUR CHURCH WORK, remember that you're working with individuals, not statistics. The story is told of a father with four daughters who waited up when they were all out one evening. The first daughter came home just before midnight, followed closely by two of her sisters. Once they were home, the father turned out the lights, locked the front door, and got ready for bed. The man's wife pointed out that their fourth daughter hadn't returned yet, but the man said, "Seventy-five percent of them are home; isn't that a pretty good percentage?"

APOSTLE MATTHEW COWLEY was asked in 1953 to speak at a BYU devotional on the subject of miracles. "It will be a miracle if I do," said Elder Cowley at the beginning of his address. He recalled some advice President George Albert Smith gave him shortly after his call to the Quorum of the Twelve.

"This is just a particular suggestion to you. Not to all the brethren, but to you," the prophet told him. "Never write a sermon. Never write down what you are going to say."

Brother Cowley answered, "What on earth will I do?"

"You tell the people what the Lord wants you to tell them while you are standing on your feet," said President Smith.

"That is certainly putting some responsibility on the Lord," said Brother Cowley—but he took the advice, and used it to greatly magnify his talents.

IN THE FEAR OF THE LORD is strong confidence," says Proverbs. Susannah White, an early settler of rural Utah, provided an example. While her husband was away for several days, she was visited by a man the locals called "the meanest Indian in the country," who asked her to put him up for the night.

"You 'fraid?" he asked. "No," she answered. "I can shoot as good as any Indian." The Indian laughed; Susannah didn't. She kept a worried eye on him until, as he crawled into his bed, he paused to kneel and say his prayers. Much relieved, she told herself, "I don't need to be afraid of a praying Indian." The next morning the Indian built her fire, cut a load of firewood, offered to milk the cows, and left two slabs of fresh venison before riding away.

Humility—and a self-effacing wit—were two prominent traits of Joseph Fielding Smith. An admiring Church member once asked him to sign his John Henry on a stake conference program. President Smith obliged; he wrote "John Henry." On another occasion, at the Logan Temple, two temple workers approached him after watching him intently for some time. "You look just like Joseph Fielding Smith," said one. President Smith acted flattered but didn't spill the beans. "I do!" he said. "Well, thank you!"

EVERY DAY, YOU HAVE THE OPTION of choosing how you'll live your life, said Sterling W. Sill in a 1971 conference talk. You can think uplifting thoughts, listen to good music, read fine literature, and do good deeds—or you can immerse yourself in rebellion, weakness, and evil.

Brother Sill told the story of a man who made wrong choices, then compounded them by dwelling on his mistakes. "He often referred to the fact that his DFT drawer was the largest file in his office," said the General Authority. "Someone once asked him what these file letters stood for, and he said they identified a collection of the damn fool things he had done."

"Most of us are not bad people," said Brother Sill. "We just let our DFT files get too large."

SOMETIMES WE HAVE TO ASK OURSELVES: In the work we're engaged in, are we part of the problem, or part of the cure? Two missionaries on a tandem bicycle—who had just huffed and puffed their way to the top of an extremely steep hill—illustrate the concept.

"Boy, that was a steep hill," said the elder in front as he dripped with perspiration. "I didn't think we'd make it."

The other missionary was much more calm. He looked behind him down the hill, then said, "I'm sure we'd have gone backwards if I hadn't had the brake on all the way up."

"TRUST IN THE LORD with all thine heart, and lean not unto thine own understanding," says Proverbs.

Abraham Lincoln illustrated his belief in this principle when he was greeting guests at a White House reception one evening during the Civil War. One of the visitors shook the president's hand and told him solemnly that the future of the country depended on God and Abraham Lincoln.

"You are half right," said the president.

NATHAN ELDON TANNER—who would become a high-ranking official in the Canadian government, a powerful business leader, an apostle, and a counselor to four prophets—didn't overly impress his dad when he was born.

Eldon was born in Salt Lake City, but his father was in Canada at the time. When the boy was not quite two months old, his mother returned to Canada, where his father saw him for the first time. Nathan William Tanner—who was noted for his ever-ready sense of humor—looked at his young son, then said to his wife, "Is that the best you can do?"

SOON AFTER THE GREAT-AUNT of Alan Ruff passed away, the boy and his mother sat down to talk about it. Alan was only two, but was unusually perceptive and had an advanced vocabulary. "Alan, honey," said his mother, Betty Clark Ruff, "Aunt Lida has gone back to Heavenly Father."

"Who took her?" Alan asked.

His mother hemmed and hawed, then said, "It must have been someone she knew."

Immediately his little face lit up. "Oh, I know what it's like," he said. "Grandpa Clark brought me when I came to you. He'll probably take me back when I die." Alan then proceeded to describe his Grandfather Clark, who had been dead nearly twelve years. He had never even seen a picture of him. He also spoke of Heavenly Father as a definite memory. For several months Alan shared his memories. "Then," said his mother, "suddenly the memory was erased and he did not know what we were talking about when we discussed it."

WHEN N. ELDON TANNER was running for a seat in the Alberta provincial legislature, representing Canada's Social Creditor party, he encountered a drunk at a campaign meeting who kept spouting his membership in a rival political faction. "I am a Liberal," said the man repeatedly. Seeking to quiet the man, Eldon asked him why he was a Liberal. "Well," said the man, "my grandfather was a Liberal, my father was a Liberal, my whole family are Liberals, and so I am a Liberal."

According to a Toronto newspaper, Eldon asked, "If your grandfather were a jackass, and your father were a jackass, and your whole family were jackasses, what would that make you?"

"A Social Creditor," said the man.

ONE WINTER WHEN Joseph Fielding Smith was president of the Quorum of the Twelve, he was scheduled to have his picture taken with a group of Primary boys on Temple Square. As they walked outside in the cold, President Smith noticed that one of the boys was shivering beneath his thin jacket. He asked the boy where his coat was; the boy said he didn't have one.

"Get inside my coat with me then, son," said President Smith, as he wrapped the boy in his own heavy coat. "We can walk together."

LATE IN DAVID O. MCKAY'S MINISTRY, after he had suffered strokes, heart attacks, and other physical setbacks, he likened his condition to a sick little boy who told his mother, "You know, I feels well, and I eats well, and I sleeps well, but I just can't work."

The mother, the prophet said, asked the boy: "You feels well?" "Yes," the boy replied. "You sleeps well?" "Yes," he said. "And you eats well?" "Yes."

"And you just can't work?"

"Nope," said the boy.

"Well, that's no disease," said his mother. "That's a gift."

A RANCHER IN KAMAS, at the base of Utah's Uinta mountains, decided he wanted to sell his ranch. He hired a real estate agent, who came out to inspect his property and write up an ad.

Later the realtor called the rancher to go over the ad copy with him before placing it in the paper. "For sale," read the realtor, "Picturesque white frame ranch house with white picket fence and eighty acres of rich farmland in the middle of beautiful Kamas Valley. Clear streams of mountain water flow nearby, well-stocked with rainbow trout. House faces rugged mountain peaks and is located in a small, friendly farming community with good schools and a new church."

"Stop!" said the rancher. "The deal's off! This is the kind of place I've wanted all my life!"

The moral: "Hold fast to the blessings which God has provided for you," said J. Reuben Clark. "Yours is not the task to gain them. They are here; yours is the part of cherishing them."

CHIEKO N. OKAZAKI TELLS THE STORY of a woman who spent $5.95 to buy an amaryllis bulb, which she planted. "Then suddenly, one day when she wasn't looking, it burst into a flamboyant, crimson flower," said Sister Okazaki. It was stunning; it was beautiful.

And it was short-lived. After the flower had withered and died, the woman thought of other things she could have purchased with her $5.95. For example, she thought, she could have bought a stainless steel spoon.

"However," said the woman, "I own a drawerful of spoons. And not one of them in five years has given me as much happiness as the amaryllis has in one week."

The woman knew the death of the amaryllis was unimportant. What is important, said Sister Okazaki, was its beauty, its vibrancy, and the joy it gave to whoever came near.

N. ELDON TANNER'S accomplishments are legendary. He was a provincial legislator and a member of the prime minister's cabinet in Canada. He was a powerful and prominent business executive. He was a bishop, stake president, Scout leader, apostle, and counselor to four prophets. He was a dedicated husband and a successful father.

He also maintained a powerful sense of humility—and of humor.

"Many times people would say to him, 'How do you accomplish so much? How do you do so many things?'" said his daughter, Ruth. "He usually replied, 'Not very well.'"

"WE SEE THINGS NOT AS THEY ARE, but as we are," said Delbert L. Stapley in a 1971 conference address.

Sterling W. Sill illustrated that thought several years later with the story of a young man who was torn by two career options: Entering the ministry or staying with his father on their farm. One day the clouds in the sky seemed to form two huge letters—a "P" and a "C"—that solved the dilemma. There was his answer, the young man thought; the Lord was telling him to "Preach Christ."

His father interpreted the revelation differently. To him, the heavenly message said: "Plant Corn."

SOON AFTER MATTHEW COWLEY was called as an apostle, J. Reuben Clark, first counselor in the First Presidency, gave him some advice: "Now, kid, don't forget rule six."

"What's rule six?" asked Elder Cowley.

"Don't take yourself too darn seriously," said President Clark.

"What are the other five?" Elder Cowley asked.

"There aren't any," said President Clark.

WHEN HOWARD W. HUNTER turned eighty, his family held a dinner in his honor. Each shared their sentiments about his most admirable qualities and the impact of his life on theirs. Then they asked for any advice he'd gained after eight decades of living.

President Hunter thought for a moment before speaking. "Well," he said gravely, "when you take a shower, keep the curtains inside the tub."

TOWARD THE END OF Hugh B. Brown's life, he was lying in a hospital bed, critically ill. Harold B. Lee, who was then president of the Church, gave him a blessing. His care providers expected him to be gone by morning's light; his family prepared a statement announcing his passing.

But the next morning, Elder Brown woke up and greeted his doctor with characteristic vigor. "I fooled you, didn't I!" he said.

ONCE WHEN SPENCER W. KIMBALL was
president of the Church, he was hospitalized
for emergency surgery, and one of his counselors, N. Eldon Tanner, took his place at
some conferences in Australia and New
Zealand.

During the trip, President Tanner called
every day for updates on the prophet's condition. After five or six days of these reports, one
day President Tanner was unable to hear an
update; the prophet wasn't in his room—and
the hospital staff didn't know where he was.

"They couldn't find him," said President
Tanner. "They thought he might have gone
down to the next floor of the hospital to visit
the sick."

HEBER J. GRANT HEARD A Primary teacher give a powerful lesson on tithing. "She brought ten beautiful apples to her class," he said. "She explained that everything we have in the world came to us from the Lord, and she said, 'Now, children, if I give one of you these ten apples, will you give me one back again?'" Everyone in the class held up their hand to show they would, said the prophet.

But adults are often another matter, he added. "The great trouble with the majority of people is that when they get the ten apples, they eat up nine of them and then they cut the other in two and give the Lord half of what is left. Some of them cut the apple in two and eat up one-half of it and then hold up the other half and ask the Lord to take a bite."

MANY YEARS AGO ONE OF THE young grandsons of Howard W. Hunter attended tithing settlement with his dad. The boy, who was just seven, told his bishop he had paid a full tithing—of fourteen cents—on his earnings that year. The bishop was pleased, and he asked the young man if he believed the Church was true.

The boy said yes, he thought it was. "But it sure costs a lot of money," he added.

ONE OF THE NEW MISSIONARIES arriving in San Diego, California, in early 1978 was a young man from rural Utah—very rural Utah. In a car packed with missionaries and luggage on a freeway that wove from the San Diego airport to the mission home, the new elder looked out at mile after mile of suburban homes. After twenty minutes of thoughtful silence he asked: "Do people *live* in all these houses?"

"Yes," said the veteran elder who was driving the car. The new elder mulled that fact over, then asked another question.

"Where do they keep their sheep?" he asked.

A SISTER NAMED LOLA WALTERS, a newly-wed, read a magazine article that counseled new husbands and wives to point out each other's annoying mannerisms. She and her husband decided to try it.

"I started off," she said. "I told him that I didn't like the way he ate grapefruit. He peeled it and ate it like an orange! Nobody else I knew ate grapefruit like that. Could a girl be expected to spend a lifetime, and even eternity, watching her husband eat grapefruit like an orange?"

Soon it was her husband's turn. "Well," he said, "to tell the truth, I can't think of anything I don't like about you, honey."

"I quickly turned my back," said Lola, "because tears had filled my eyes and were running down my face. Whenever I hear of married couples being incompatible, I always wonder if they are suffering from what I now call 'the Grapefruit Syndrome.'"

· AUGUST 5 ·

SPENCER W. KIMBALL'S EVERY ACT reflected
a number of virtues. Among them: humility—
and the desire to carry his own weight.

President Kimball was in an airport in
Copenhagen, Denmark, carrying his luggage
down the long airport halls, when James O.
Mason, a physician and future member of the
Seventy who was traveling with the prophet,
offered to help with his bags. "No, thank
you," said President Kimball. "I have to have
a reason for being here."

EZRA TAFT BENSON SERVED as Secretary of
Agriculture under President Dwight D.
Eisenhower—but he didn't stray far from his
roots on an Idaho farm. Once a group of
reporters prodded the citified secretary into
milking a cow. "I took my position, grinned at
them, and told them to stand back or I'd
squirt milk on them," he said. "They backed
about ten feet away. I overheard one reporter
say, 'He'll never reach us here.'

"Oh yeah, I thought," said the U.S.
Secretary of Agriculture. "And when I got
going pretty well, I suddenly shot a spray of
milk and got him good, and some of the cam-
eras, too."

WHEN GEORGE ALBERT SMITH took sick, his physician administered a new drug made of sulfa that produced a reaction almost as bad as the original malady. The doctor said such reactions weren't uncommon. "We have learned that one of twelve can't tolerate sulfa," he said.

"That's right," replied President Smith. "You see, I'm one of the Twelve."

WHEN DAVID O. MCKAY was far advanced in age, he shared an elevator ride in the Hotel Utah with a young boy who shook his hand with adoration and awe. The boy got off the elevator a level below the prophet's floor, but when President McKay exited the elevator and walked slowly toward his apartment, there in the hall was the boy again, extending his hand again toward the prophet and breathing hard after a run up the stairs.

"I just wanted to shake hands with you once more before you die," said the boy.

A YOUNG MAN IN PRISON battled boredom by reading anything he could find. "One day I saw a fellow with a nice, thick book," he remembered. "I knew it would take a long time to read, so I offered him my pork chops, my potatoes, and all my main course food items for a week. He accepted my offer and loaned me the book. As I read it, I knew I was reading something very special and very true. The book for which I had sacrificed my food was the Book of Mormon.

"When I had a chance, I found the missionaries, changed my habits, and am now finding a new way of life. I love that book for which I traded my food."

WHEN WILLIAM HOWELLS LEFT his native Wales in 1849 to serve as the Church's first missionary in France, his preaching was met with great success—and great hostility. One man pounded on the door of the missionary's apartment one morning. "Trembling with passion, grinding his teeth, and shaking his clenched fist in my face," Brother Howells recorded, the man said he'd break every bone in the missionary's body unless he stopped preaching and distributing tracts.

But Brother Howells kept the faith. "He had never tried, I suppose, the toughness of a Welshman's bones," he said.

ONCE WHEN DAVID O. MCKAY was in New York, the United Press wanted some pictures of the Mormon prophet. The regular photographer was unavailable, however, so a crime photographer—who was used to seeing the harshest elements of the city—was sent. The man took longer on the assignment than expected, shot and developed much more film than was needed, and defended his actions vigorously when he was questioned. A United Press executive eventually summoned the man to his office to ask why he had responded to his assignment in such a way.

"When I was a little boy, my mother used to read to me out of the Old Testament, and all my life I have wondered what a prophet of God must really look like," said the crime photographer. "Well, today I found one."

HOPING TO SHAME HIM into cleaning up his language, a woman once asked J. Golden Kimball if he'd ever heard Heber J. Grant—the president of the Church—swear.

Just once, said J. Golden. The two were in St. George one summer, during a drought, when the crops were withering and the Saints were facing a bleak harvest. The two Church leaders joined the local members in a prayer for rain, but no rain came.

"I said, 'It's a d——d shame!'" said J. Golden, "and President Grant said, 'Yes, it is.'"

THINK ABOUT THIS WHEN IT'S TIME to do your home teaching: George Q. Cannon had just returned from a mission to Hawaii when he was called to publish a newspaper in Fillmore in central Utah. Five months later a messenger from Salt Lake City delivered the apostle a note. It was another mission call from Brigham Young; Elder Cannon's mission to the eastern United States was to begin the next day.

How did he respond? "I gathered up what clothing and bedding and weapons I needed for the journey, and in about three quarters of an hour we were on our way," he wrote. "As I had only been home from a mission a few weeks before I went to Fillmore . . . I had no home in Salt Lake City. In leaving my family at the roadside, therefore, I left them with no bright prospects for comfort and ease during my absence. But they uttered no complaints. They put their trust in the Lord and during the two years of my absence, He was their benefactor and friend."

ELDER MATTHEW COWLEY ONCE was on his way from Tahiti to New Zealand. The earliest departing ship was a freighter that wasn't allowed to take passengers, so he joined the ship's crew. "I never did find out what my duties were," he said. "I thought for a time that I might be the chaplain, but we crossed the international date line Saturday night, and when I woke up it was Monday, so Sunday was scratched right out."

Once the ship reached its destination, the missionary knew what his calling was—and what it wasn't. "Before they started doing the heavy work of unloading the ship," said Elder Cowley, "I signed off as a member of the crew."

BRIGHAM YOUNG was a plainspoken man, and he appreciated that trait in others. Once, in presenting the leaders of the Church to be sustained, he started with his own name. "If any person can say that he should not be sustained in this office, say so," Brother Brigham said. "If there is no objection . . . let them forever afterward hold their peace, and not go sniveling around, saying that they would like to have a better man."

WHEN WILLIAM FLAKE WAS CALLED in 1877 to help the Saints settle northern Arizona, he bought a ranch from James Stinson, a non-member. Mr. Stinson counseled the settler to hoard his water; there was enough for the ranch, but not enough for the rest of the valley. Sharing the water would mean everyone in the valley would starve, he said. Brother Flake, who was planning a new Mormon town in the valley, wasn't convinced. "When the Mormons come," he said, "the water will increase."

Soon afterward it started raining in the valley, and so much rain came that Mr. Stinson couldn't harvest all of his crops. His comment to Brother Flake: "I wish the h— the Mormons had stayed away until I had my crop gathered."

So you're not perfect? You're in good company.

Joseph Fielding Smith, for all his abilities, never progressed beyond very rudimentary typing skills. He did his typing according to what he called "the biblical system—seek and ye shall find."

JAMES'S COUNSEL—Be ye doers of the word, and not hearers only—was reflected by the Prophet Joseph Smith when the Saints were settling in Nauvoo. During a visit with a brother whose house had been burned down, a number of Saints expressed sorrow and condolences to the man.

But the prophet drew five dollars out of his pocket and expressed his sympathy with words and cash. "I feel sorry for this brother to the amount of five dollars," he said to those who were gathered around. "How much do you feel sorry?"

J. GOLDEN KIMBALL WAS BOTH LOVED and lambasted for the range of his vocabulary. Once, during the Depression, a banker gave him some advice about cleaning up his language, but J. Golden didn't appreciate the man's helpfulness. "I don't think this is a time," he said, "for bankers to be giving advice to anybody."

A BUSINESS-ORIENTED PEP RALLY in San Diego, California, in 1978 featured such noted speakers as radio commentator Paul Harvey, the Reverend Robert Schuller, and super salesman Zig Ziglar. It also featured an opening prayer by Hartman Rector, Jr., of the Seventy, who was serving as president of the San Diego mission at the time.

The themes of the conference were positive thinking and personal success.

So which is more powerful: Positive thinking—or prayer?

At the end of the conference, a drawing for a $1,000 prize was held among the several thousand people in the huge convention center.

The winner? Elder Rector.

In 1984, HOWARD W. HUNTER was in an airport in Taipei, Taiwan, in the middle of a typhoon. Thinking that the air above the storm was calm enough to fly in, the pilot took off as scheduled, and, after some initial jitters, the journey was uneventful. "Getting there was half the fun!" said Elder Hunter after the plane touched down.

"Maybe the apostle was teaching us something," said a traveling companion. "We can rise above the storm—and we should enjoy life's journey."

Effort and achievement and endurance make the difference in our lives, said Matthew Cowley in a 1953 talk at BYU. "The greatest achievement to me," he said, "is coming to the end of one's day, having been true and loyal to one's ideals. I can think of no achievement greater than that."

WHEN EZRA TAFT BENSON was Secretary of Agriculture under President Dwight D. Eisenhower, he served as a private citizen, not an apostle—but he didn't hide his apostolic light under a bushel. He encouraged President Eisenhower to begin cabinet meetings with prayer, for example, and he and his wife didn't serve liquor at social gatherings in their home.

And when Texas was parched by drought in 1953, he encouraged the state's governor to hold a statewide day of fasting and prayer. Within a few days, the governor sent Brother Benson a note saying the drought was over: The state had received two inches of rain. The governor also sent a newspaper clipping. Its headline: "Benson Really Has Contacts."

Richard L. Evans once addressed an intriguing question in conference: Should the commandments be rewritten? The definitive answer: No, they should be re-read.

During the same conference, Sterling W. Sill underscored the point. He told the story of a man who told his friend he'd give him five dollars if he could quote any one of the ten commandments.

The friend accepted the challenge. He thought long and hard, and then said: "Now I lay me down to sleep. I pray the Lord my soul to keep. If I should die before I wake, I pray the Lord my soul to take."

His friend was astounded. "Here's the money," he said. "I didn't think you could do it."

Hartman Rector, Jr., and his wife,
Connie, had been members of the Church
only sixteen years when they were asked to
come to Salt Lake City to visit with David O.
McKay. Also waiting for an interview with the
prophet were Loren C. and Sharon L. Dunn.
At the time, Brother Dunn was first counselor
in the presidency of the New England
Mission. His father-in-law was Elder John
Longden, an assistant to the Twelve. Brother
Dunn was a graduate of BYU and a returned
missionary; he had a master's degree from
Boston University and had been working in
Boston as director of communications for the
New England Council for Economic
Development.

"If you two are interviewing for the same
job," said Sister Rector to her husband as they
waited for the prophet, "we'll be on the first
plane home."

A POSITIVE MENTAL ATTITUDE is impor-
tant—and so is a firm grip on reality. Charles
Ora Card was called by President John Taylor
to build a Mormon settlement in western
Canada in 1887. The town he founded—
Cardston, in the province of Alberta—became
a wonderful settlement, but on the high
Canadian plains, it was wind-swept and cold.

One gusty, frigid morning, Brother Card
was walking to Church with his father. "Isn't
the air fresh and invigorating?" he asked.

"Yes," said his father, "and isn't there a lot
of it?"

WHAT WE DO ECHOES LOUDER than what we say, said Elder Sterling W. Sill. On a family trip to Arizona years ago, he stopped at a gas station to buy soda pop for his children. He put in a dime and got a bottle of pop; then put in two more dimes and got two more bottles; then, without inserting a dime, got a fourth bottle free. As Elder Sill walked the pop over to his children, he thought, "They charge too much for this stuff anyway."

"However," he said, "I have a little mental night watchman on duty up here in my brain someplace who started to make a fuss, and he said, 'Look, Sterling, if you're going to be a crook, you had better get more than ten cents out of it.'"

Before driving away, Elder Sill left another dime for the fourth bottle of soda.

SOON AFTER SHARLENE WELLS, a twenty-year-old BYU coed, was crowned Miss America in 1984, her father, Robert E. Wells—a member of the Seventy—was shopping in a Salt Lake City department store. "I presented my credit card to make a purchase," said Elder Wells. "The clerk looked at my identification and said, 'Robert E. Wells. Are you Miss America's father?'

"With a display of some pride, I said I was," reported Elder Wells.

"The clerk looked down again at my card, then back up at my weather-beaten face and said, 'She must have a beautiful mother.'"

MATTHEW COWLEY—who was just seventeen when he was called on a mission to New Zealand—learned at a young age to enjoy whatever successes he encountered.

He also learned that his closest companions in the mission field, based on how devotedly they stuck with him, were fleas. One of his journal entries describes how he coated himself and his bedding with flea powder one night—and the powerful result. "On arising and looking in the bed [the next morning], I found the carcasses of a multitude of fleas," he wrote. "It made me feel like Napoleon to be the victor of such a battle."

MARK TWAIN MAY BE BETTER KNOWN for his cynicism than for his values—but some of his values bear notice. A ruthless and cold-blooded East Coast business leader told the famous author that he was planning a trip to the Holy Land. "I will climb Mount Sinai and read the Ten Commandments aloud at the top," said the man.

"I have a better idea," said Twain. "You could stay home in Boston and keep them."

JOSEPH F. MERRILL, AN APOSTLE from 1931 to 1952, related a story of two bishops and two sets of boys. The first group pulled a prank at Halloween, and their bishop responded by publicly calling on them to ask forgiveness—or face Church discipline. "In consequence, there are in that community today a number of families that grew up outside the Church," said Elder Merrill.

The second group of boys engaged in a similar prank: They stole the ice cream from a wedding reception at the bishop's house. Their bishop responded by inviting them to a party—at which more ice cream was served. "When the lads were seated at the feast, it was noticed that tears began to run down one boy's face," Elder Merrill said. "Soon all the other boys were in tears also.

"From among that group," he said, "have come some of the finest leaders in their community."

Dᴀᴠɪᴅ O. Mᴄᴋᴀʏ ᴅɪᴅ ᴇᴠᴇʀʏᴛʜɪɴɢ with zest and enthusiasm. That included being seasick, said a traveling companion who accompanied the apostle on a cruise to Japan in 1920. "Brother McKay, being the leader of this tour, maintained his supremacy in the matter of seasickness as in all other things," wrote Hugh J. Cannon. "He does nothing by halves, but treats every subject exhaustively, going to the very bottom of it, and this occasion was no exception."

DURING WORLD WAR I, an English immigration officer denied John A. Widtsoe permission to enter England. The officer said Mormon missionaries could enter the country, but not their leaders. Then the man reconsidered and asked the apostle a question. "If I let you land in my country," he said, "what will you teach my people?"

"I will teach them where they came from, why they are here, and where they are going," answered Elder Widtsoe.

"Does your church teach that?" asked the immigration officer.

"It does," said the apostle.

"Well, mine doesn't," he said. He stamped Elder Widtsoe's passport. "You may enter."

ONE OF THE LORD'S PRECEPTS from the Sermon on the Mount—"Where your treasure is, there will your heart be also"—was illustrated dramatically in two journal entries made by a father and a son. The entry from Charles Francis Adams, a busy and prominent attorney, politician, and ambassador: "Went fishing with my son today—a day wasted."

On the same day, Adams's son also made a note in his journal: "Went fishing with my father today. The most wonderful day of my life."

"ALL THINGS ARE POSSIBLE to him that believeth," says Mark in the New Testament. In a talk at BYU, Norma B. Ashton compared that conviction to the sentiment printed on the shirt of a young man she walked past in a shopping mall.

"When he got close enough," she said, "I could read these words on the front of his T-shirt: 'I'd try having a positive mental attitude.' As he moved on past me, I saw these words on the back of the shirt: 'But I know it won't work.'"

IN ADDITION TO HAVING CHARITY for others, said Chieko N. Okazaki, first counselor in the general Relief Society presidency, save some for yourself. She remembered frosting a cake late one night for a homemaking lunch the next day. She'd had a long day at her job and a busy evening with her family; she was exhausted. And she knew she'd have to get up early the next morning and really hustle in order to drop off the cake and still get to work on time.

"At that moment, I had a profound revelation," she said. "The revelation was, 'This is crazy!'

"That revelation gave me enough knowledge and insight so that, the next time a similar situation came up, I could say, 'I'm sorry. I just can't right now, but I'd like to another time.'"

BYU FOOTBALL COACH LaVell Edwards told a story about a writer in Oakland, California, who was doing an article on Jack London, author of *Call of the Wild* and other noted works. The writer was looking for reactions to a passage written by London, and he approached Kenny Stabler, who was then quarterback of the NFL's Oakland Raiders.

The writer showed Stabler this quote from Jack London: "I'd rather be ashes than dust. I'd rather my flame go out in a burning spark than to be stifled with dry rot. I'd rather be a splendid meteor blazing across the sky, every atom in me in magnificent glow, than be a sleepy and permanent planet. Life is to be lived, not to exist. I shall not waste my days trying to prolong them. I will use my time."

The writer asked Stabler: "What does that mean to you?"

"Throw deep," said the quarterback.

BRUCE R. MCCONKIE AND HIS WIFE had a long conversation one evening about the blessings they enjoyed as a result of their membership in the Church. They talked about their family and all the bounties and privileges the restored gospel had provided. At the end of the discussion, Sister McConkie asked her husband to name his greatest blessing.

"Without a moment's hesitation," said Elder McConkie, "I said, 'The greatest blessing that has ever come to me was on the 13th day of October in 1937 at 11:20 A.M. when I was privileged to kneel in the Salt Lake Temple at the Lord's altar and receive you as an eternal companion.'"

"Well," replied his wife, "you passed that test."

MARION G. ROMNEY WORKED as a lawyer before he joined the Quorum of the Twelve. Early in his career he wondered if the demands of his profession could be reconciled with his commitment to the gospel. His concern was reflected in a story he told about a man in a cemetery who stopped to read a headstone that said: "Here lies John Brown, a lawyer and an honest man."

"I wonder," asked the man, "why they buried all three of them in the same grave?"

NAN GREENE HUNTER, a daughter-in-law of Howard W. Hunter, recalled a period of especially steep challenges her family once faced. One day during that time, Nan made a special effort to seek the Lord's help. "We needed to be reassured of his love and know that he remembered us in our time of trial," she said.

At the end of the day, she came home to find a blinking light on their answering machine. "Hello, Nan," said the first message. "I don't have any business to talk over. I am just thinking about you and wanted to call and say hello. This is your friend."

"Love filled me as I heard the voice of my dear father-in-law," Nan said. "I knew my prayer had been heard and a faithful servant, in tune and ready, had responded to the promptings of him who loves us all."

FACING THE TRUTH ISN'T ALWAYS EASY, but it's important, said Sterling W. Sill in 1975. He illustrated with the story of a vagrant who was charged with a crime. The man was arraigned before a judge who asked him to declare whether he was guilty or not guilty.

The vagrant wasn't ready to face the truth. He responded: "How can I tell, your honor, until I have heard the evidence?"

SOMEHOW IT'S EASIER to be your brother's keeper if you're not keeping your . . . brother. When Hugh B. Brown was very young, he and his older brother, Bud, chased a weasel into its hole, then got a shovel and started to dig it out. "We dug down quite a ways," Elder Brown recalled, "and Bud said, 'I think I can hear him down there; we are pretty close to him. Maybe you'd better reach in and see what he's doing.'

"I rolled up my sleeve and reached down into the hole," said Elder Brown. "I still have a scar."

BYU PROFESSOR AND popular speaker George Durrant told the story of a traveler who stopped in Manti in central Utah to ask for directions. "How do I get to Salt Lake City from here?" he asked.

The farmer outlined two options: Left to Moroni, then up to Nephi, then north to Salt Lake—or up to the turnoff at Thistle, down Spanish Fork Canyon, then north to Salt Lake.

The driver paused while he thought about the two options. "Does it matter which way I go?" he asked.

"Not to me," said the farmer.

A SPARROW CANNOT FALL to the ground without the Lord being aware of it, says the Bible. So it was with David O. McKay. Once, after some saddles had been stolen from the prophet's tack shed near Huntsville, some family members noticed a window in the shed was open, so they shut it before locking the shed. They later mentioned the open window to President McKay, but he was well aware of it. He'd noticed a bird's nest inside the shed, he said; he left the window open so the parents could bring food to the baby birds inside.

President McKay immediately returned to the shed to reopen the window. "It was just as I expected," he reported. "One little bird was outside trying to get in, and the mother was inside attempting to get out."

Dᴜʀɪɴɢ ᴀ ᴅɪɴɴᴇʀ ᴘᴀʀᴛʏ honoring LeGrand Richards on his ninetieth birthday, N. Eldon Tanner asked the aged but irrepressibly enthusiastic apostle if he'd lived all of his life in the United States.

"Not yet!" said Brother Richards.

HUGH B. BROWN'S great-grandson sat on his lap once, saw his white hair and lined face, and asked, "Grandpa Brown, were you on Noah's ark?" President Brown said, no, he wasn't on the ark. "Well," asked the little boy, "how come you weren't drowned?"

SOMETIMES YOU SHOULDN'T ASK what you can do to help someone, you just need to do it, said Chieko N. Okazaki, first counselor in the general Relief Society presidency. She told the story of an aged widow, suffering from arthritis, who was visited by her bishopric in the middle of the winter. "The snow on her front sidewalk was so deep that they were soaked to the knees by the time they got to her door. She welcomed them in, and as they sat in her living room, the bishop asked, 'Well, Sister So-and-so, is there anything we can do for you?'

"She didn't say," said Sister Okazaki, "what she was thinking: 'Bishop, what did you just wade through to get into my house? Does that give you a clue?'"

In the 1880s, about the time that John Morgan was released as president of the Southern States Mission, twenty-seven missionaries were on a train going to Tennessee. According to Elder J. Golden Kimball, who was one of the twenty-seven, the "hard-looking" elders preached, talked, sang, "and advertised loudly their calling as preachers." Their behavior attracted the attention of an older man on the train. "The elders soon commenced a discussion and argument with the stranger, and before he got through they were in grave doubt about their message of salvation," said Elder Kimball. "He gave them a training that they never forgot."

The stranger was B. H. Roberts, the prominent Mormon scholar and theologian—who was the southern states' new mission president.

ACCORDING TO ONE HISTORIAN, Brigham Young was "a handsome, portly gentleman with . . . radiant blue eyes, a square set jaw, and a pleasant expression on his face." Another witness—the young daughter of pioneer Anson Call—disagreed. Sitting on his lap one night, she studied him for a time, then rendered her opinion. "Your eyes," she told the prophet, "look just like our sow's!"

As a missionary, Lorenzo Snow preached one winter night to a group of people in a farmhouse. The group included several members of an anti-Mormon mob who planned to attack Elder Snow as soon as he left the house. After the meeting, however, Elder Snow happened to stand close to one of the thugs, and the man's hand brushed against a bulky, heavy object in the missionary's coat pocket. He assumed it was a pistol and hurried outside to warn his cohorts that the Mormon was armed. The mob scattered.

But there was no pistol in Lorenzo Snow's pocket. It was a pocket Bible given to him by the Prophet Joseph Smith.

TIME WAS PRECIOUS to Joseph Fielding Smith. He wore a watch on each wrist, owned two back-up watches in case of emergency, and rose early every morning. "People die in bed," he said. "And so does ambition."

"Somehow it seemed immoral to lie in bed after six," said one of his sons. "Of course, I only tried it once. Father saw to that."

PRESIDENT SPENCER W. KIMBALL was on a
tour of Europe when a change in his schedule
made it possible for him to hold an extra
meeting with all the missionaries in a
European mission. But when the prophet
arrived at the appointed place, he found the
meeting hadn't been scheduled. His personal
secretary and the mission president explained
they were concerned about overly taxing
President Kimball's strength. His response
teaches a lesson to every member of the
Church.

"You're trying to save me," said the
prophet, "but I don't want to be saved. I want
to be exalted."

ELAINE CANNON, former general president of the Young Women, told a true story about a three-year-old boy who wandered away from home one day and ended up crying and cold on the porch of a young Latter-day Saint woman. The young woman alerted the police, who started a search for the boy's mother, then she wrapped the boy in a blanket and sang soothing songs to him while he sat in her lap. The young woman made the lost child feel marvelous, said Sister Cannon. They drew pictures; they ate ice cream cones.

Finally the boy's mother came—and as the boy left, he had a question for his wonderful hostess. "Hey," he said, "are you Heavenly Father's wife?"

"No," said the young woman after a pause. "I'm his daughter."

Ann Edwards Cannon, the daughter of
BYU football coach LaVell Edwards, said that
when her dad was a high school senior in
Orem, Utah, he was a dedicated, but not an
especially talented, member of a mixed chorus. During a Christmas rendition of Handel's
Messiah, "instead of singing the required four
hallelujahs and then pausing, Dad always sang
a fifth enthusiastic hallelujah," his daughter
said.

Eventually the exasperated choir leader, in
a private visit with LaVell, said he'd earn an
"A" if he would promise to mouth the words
during the chorus's performance. "Dad is the
only person I know," said Ann, "who managed to pass a singing class without making a
sound."

On a trip to New York, Elder Bernard P. Brockbank sat by a businessman who explained the philosophy he'd adopted as his personal religion: Moderation in all things.

"How does it work in 'Thou shalt not kill'?" asked Elder Brockbank. "Just a little killing?"

In 1905, ANDREW KIMBALL watched his ten-year-old son, Spencer, as the boy milked a cow and sang a hymn at the top of his lungs. "That boy, Spencer, is an exceptional boy," said Andrew to a neighbor. "He always tries to mind me, whatever I ask him to do. I have dedicated him to be one of the mouthpieces of the Lord, the Lord willing. You will see him some day as a great leader. He will become a mighty man in the Church."

And all the cow-milking the boy did came in handy, too. Sixty-eight years later, when Spencer became president of the Church, he said, "I milked cows all my life so I could shake hands. I don't get tired."

Marion G. Romney shared an updated version of the Savior's sermon about the beam and the mote. President Romney once wanted his wife to see her doctor for a hearing check up, but Sister Romney didn't think she needed to. So, in consultation with her doctor, President Romney devised a plan to convince his wife she needed her hearing checked.

He stood at their home's front door and called, "Ida!" She didn't respond. He stepped inside and called again. But again there was no response. He tried a third time from the dining room, and still there was no reply. Finally, he walked into the kitchen and told Sister Romney that he'd called to her three times.

"I know, my dear," she said, "and I have answered you three times."

A light bulb clicked on. "The problem," said President Romney, "wasn't Ida's."

WHEN HEBER J. GRANT was just twenty-four, he was called to be president of the Tooele Stake—and despite his youthfulness, he taught a lesson speakers today might remember. After he was sustained as stake president, he delivered a sermon that was extremely short. Why? "I ran out of ideas," he said.

MARVIN J. ASHTON LEARNED a wonderful lesson from a cab driver early one morning in San Francisco. His parents lived in New Mexico, the talkative driver said, but they loved to visit him and his brother and their grandchildren in the Bay Area. Their trips were especially enriching because the San Francisco weather seemed to boost his mother's health; at home in New Mexico, her strength seemed to flag.

So the cab driver decided what he had to do. "I found a large truck, and my brother and I drove to New Mexico," he told Elder Ashton. "We loaded our parents and all their possessions into the truck, and brought them to live near those who loved them most. Mother's health improved noticeably.

"You know," said the cabbie, "love is very important if it is done right."

THE LAW OF THE SABBATH was tested some
years ago by a farmer in Ohio who singled out
ten acres of his land and worked it—plowed,
planted, cultivated, and harvested—exclusively
on the Sabbath. By the end of October, the
man discovered his Sabbath-only acres produced a richer harvest per acre than any other
part of his farm. He sent a letter to the *Toledo
Blade* explaining his experiment and boasting
of his discovery.

The paper printed the letter, but ran a
short note from a wise editor at the end:
"Remember, my brother, God Almighty does
not always settle his accounts in October."

WILLARD L. JONES WAS A stake president, a
state legislator, and a farmer in southern
Nevada in the early 1900s. And he was a
pretty fast runner. One moonlit night he
heard some whispering out in his melon patch
and saw a group of boys—all members of his
stake—rummaging for ripe watermelons.

When he stepped outside, the boys scattered and fled, and the stake president gave
chase. He ran fast enough to identify almost
all of the boys, but not fast enough to collar
them.

The next day President Jones passed one
of the boys on the way to town. His response
teaches all of us an important lesson about forgiveness. He tipped his hat, grinned, and said,
"Nice run we had last night!"

WHEN DAVID O. MCKAY SAID, "No success can compensate for failure in the home," he may have been thinking of one of his counselors. At one time in his life, N. Eldon Tanner was the head of two major divisions of the Canadian national government, a minister in the cabinet of that country's prime minister, president of Canada's Boy Scout Association, a branch president—and a husband and a dad.

Brother Tanner did his family's wash, got up with his children if they were sick, cooked breakfast every morning—and shared his priorities with his associates at work. "At the age of eight," said his daughter, Helen, "my girlfriend and I put our dolls in their carriages and walked the several blocks to the government building. Daddy's secretary announced us, and we were introduced to the men he was meeting with. We introduced our dolls and were thanked for coming."

JOSEPH FIELDING SMITH and Jessie Evans were married in 1938 in the Salt Lake Temple by Heber J. Grant. "Now, Joseph, kiss your wife," said President Grant as the ceremony ended.

Thirty-three years later, President Smith recounted his obedience to his predecessor's counsel. "He said it like he meant it," he said, "and I have been doing it ever since."

Heber J. Grant's persistence is legendary. During his life, he overcame significant shortages of natural ability to learn to sing, play baseball, and improve his penmanship. His handwriting was an especially steep hill to climb. Two of his young boyhood friends pointed out his deficiencies once, he recalled. "That writing looks like hen tracks," one said. "No," said the other, "it looks as if lightning had struck an ink bottle."

The result: Young Heber slammed his fist down and vowed that someday he'd be qualified to teach lessons in penmanship. Years later, he was.

DAVID O. McKAY once was called away from his office suddenly and had to miss an appointment with the young members of a Sunday School class who had come to see him. One of the apostles met with the children in President McKay's place; the visit ended as successfully as possible.

The next Sunday morning, as the class met in their Salt Lake City chapel, the door to their classroom opened, and in stepped President McKay. "I want you children to know," he said, "that the president of the Church keeps his appointments if at all possible."

LOOKING FOR AN EXAMPLE of an effective—and enthusiastic—missionary? Floriano Oliveira, a Brazilian high councilor who has baptized over 200 people, was driving in Sao Paulo one day when he became distracted momentarily and ran into the car in front of him. Brother Oliveira ran up to the other driver's door and said, "I am so sorry I hit you. It was all my fault. I accept the full blame and will pay the total costs. I had no intention to do this, so please forgive me. Yet if I hadn't hit you, you wouldn't have received this message I have for you, the message you have waited for all your life . . ."

Two weeks later, the driver of the other car was baptized.

REMEMBER THE DIFFERENCE between being thrifty and being cheap. "The laborer is worthy of his hire," says Luke, the apostle and physician.

That thought is illustrated by the story of another physician, 2,000 years later, who ran into a man at a party one night. The man started describing some symptoms he'd suffered recently and asking what they might be. The doctor wrote a name on a card and gave it to the man.

"What's this?" said the man.

The doctor said: "That's the name of some people who are throwing a party next week. They're inviting a specialist who's familiar with your symptoms."

TWO ARE BETTER THAN ONE," says Ecclesi-astes. "For if they fall, the one will lift up his fellow, but woe to him that is alone when he falleth, for he hath not another to help him up."

Marvin J. Ashton provided an example with the story of a newly called member of a stake presidency who was inactive when he was young. "My wife has had much to do with this special calling that is now mine," said the man. "When we were dating and I was inactive in the Church, I gained the courage one night to ask her if she would marry me. She didn't say yes and she didn't say no. She said, 'Where?'"

The man spent a good part of a year preparing himself to take his bride to the temple. "She had made her plans, and I loved her enough to rechart my course to coincide with hers. I knew what to do and where I had to go if I wanted to travel at her side."

REMEMBER THIS WISDOM from David O. McKay the next time you need to do your home teaching: The callings you have are less important than how well you fill them. In the eyes of the Lord, the home teacher and the mission president are probably equals.

AFTER GROWING UP IN RURAL Sanpete County, Utah, in the early 1900s, Joe Bischoff eventually became a bishop and a temple worker. But when he was a teenager, Brother Bischoff's potential wasn't always apparent.

One night at an MIA meeting, he was called on to give an extemporaneous talk. He walked up to the pulpit, looked out at the congregation, paused, looked at the congregation some more, then walked back down to his seat without saying a word.

"It was the shortest talk I ever gave," he said years later, "and I don't know but that it wasn't the best."

BYU PROFESSOR AND popular speaker George Durrant told the story of two young hunters who shot a deer, then grabbed it by its hind legs and started dragging it through the woods to their camp. As they pulled the deer along the ground, they ran across a much more experienced hunter. "You know," said the older man, "dragging that deer would be easier if you dragged him by his antlers so you'd be going with the grain of his fur." The two young hunters thought for a minute, then grabbed the deer's antlers and gave a tug. After a mile or two, one said, "The old guy was right. This is a lot easier."

"Yeah," said the other one, "the only problem is, we're getting further and further from camp."

In 1933, HEBER J. GRANT appreciated the growing respect the Church and its members were earning. "Today the word 'Mormon' is a certificate of character in all parts of the United States and in many other parts of the world where we are known," said the prophet.

He illustrated this with the story of a man who sought to ridicule the Saints. "You people are always happy," said the man. "If a man hits a Mormon and knocks him down, the Mormon thanks the Lord because he needed a little chastisement. And if you hit at a Mormon and miss him, he thanks the Lord for not getting hit."

Brigham Young encouraged Utah's early Saints to support local merchants and craftsmen. Years later, Heber J. Grant endorsed the same idea by telling a story about an early member of the Church.

Brother Farrell was on his way to conference when he ran into a man who had made some shoes for Brother Farrell's children, and to whom he owed five dollars. "He gave this brother the five dollars," President Grant said, "and *he* turned around and handed the money to another brother whom he owed, and he handed it to another, and he handed it to another, and the fourth brother came up and handed it back to Brother Farrell, saying, 'I owe you six dollars; here is five of it,' and Brother Farrell put the money back into his pocket.

"That money paid 500 percent in debt there," said President Grant, "in just about the same length of time that it takes me to tell the story."

DURING WORLD WAR I, Heber J. Grant was involved with a national group of businessmen who were working to sell war bonds. When the group met in California, many of its members expressed grave concern that America and her allies wouldn't win the war.

President Grant set them straight. "I said, 'So far as the Mormons are concerned, we have no fear whatever as to the outcome. Every Mormon believes in the Book of Mormon, and the Book of Mormon teaches that this is a land choice above all other lands, and that no king—or kaiser for that matter—will ever reign here.'"

How did the group respond? "Several said, 'My gracious, we had better join the Mormon church,'" said President Grant.

IN 1953 MATTHEW COWLEY visited a hospital to give a blessing to a young boy in an iron lung who suffered from polio and pneumonia. Two weeks later he visited the boy again, and before he left, the boy asked him to give a similar blessing to the boy's roommate, who also had polio. Two weeks after that, Elder Cowley dropped by the hospital a third time and found his little friend feeling sad and lonely.

"Maybe I shouldn't have asked you to bless my partner," said the boy. "He got well so soon and has gone home."

ENDURE TO THE END, said Robert L. Simpson. No matter how shaky things are at first, keep going. One example: his first high school football game. His coach sent him into the game at halftime; Elder Simpson was to kick off before 6,000 screaming fans. "I was going to kick that ball farther than any football had ever been kicked in history," he said. He remembers his entire body tingling with excitement; he remembers charging down the field. And then what?

"I missed the ball," said Elder Simpson. "But that wasn't the half of it. This was back in the days when the quarterback held the ball with his finger. I broke the quarterback's finger."

What happened next? He didn't quit. The coach left him in. "I played the rest of the game," he said. "If I weren't so modest, I might also tell you that I made all-league that year."

MATTHEW COWLEY TOLD THE STORY of a convert—a newly ordained priest—who served in the U.S. Navy. Whenever his ship came into port, the sailor's crewmates went out on the town while the LDS sailor stayed behind. "On Sunday, the captain of the ship gives me a little room, and I go into that room all by myself," the sailor said. "I have that little serviceman's copy of the Book of Mormon, so I take a little water and a piece of bread. I open up that Book of Mormon to Moroni, and I get down on my knees. I bless the sacrament, and I pass it to myself. Then," he added, "I am safe for another week."

· OCTOBER 17 ·

In 1921, THE NEWLY SUSTAINED apostle David O. McKay stopped in Hilo, Hawaii, as part of a world tour to many of the far-flung outposts of the Church. After a conference, Elder McKay and several local members climbed to the lip of one of Hilo's active volcanoes to look down into its fiery crater. While the crater's heat was formidable, the wind blowing outside the crater was chilling, so Elder McKay and three others climbed down to a small ledge inside the volcano, where they were protected from the wind.

After some time on the ledge, Elder McKay suddenly said, "Brethren, I feel impressed that we should get out of here." As soon as they were safely off the ledge—"almost immediately," said an eyewitness—the whole balcony crumbled and fell with a roar into the molten lava a hundred feet or so below.

"To us," said the witness, "it was a direct revelation given to a worthy man."

HEBER C. KIMBALL and his son, J. Golden, both were prone to quote scripture out of context. "After I get through quoting, you wouldn't recognize it," said J. Golden. His father, who was a counselor to Brigham Young, took the same approach when he cited a scriptural reference, only he went a step further. "Well," said Heber once, "if that isn't in the Bible, it ought to be in it."

LUCILE C. READING, A FORMER counselor in the general Primary presidency and managing editor of *The Friend* magazine, illustrated her belief in the joys of work with a story about Thomas Edison.

Edison's wife worried her husband was working too hard and encouraged him to take a vacation.

"But where would I go?" asked the inventor.

"Just decide where you'd rather be than anywhere else on earth, and then go there," Mrs. Edison advised.

Her husband agreed. "Very well," he said. "I will go there tomorrow."

The next morning found him right back in his laboratory.

BEFORE THE MORMONS CAME, Nauvoo was a swamp. After they came, it became one again for two children who were walking to school on a muddy Nauvoo road the day after a rainstorm. The mud was so thick, and the children were so small, they soon couldn't walk without leaving their shoes behind—and they expressed their misery to the heavens. Their wails were answered by a tall, cheerful man who lifted them onto dry ground, scraped the mud from their shoes, then dabbed at their tears with his handkerchief.

"He spoke kind and cheering words to us," wrote one of the children later, "and sent us on our way to school rejoicing."

Their benefactor was the Prophet Joseph Smith.

U.S. SENATOR ORRIN HATCH took one of his Senate colleagues on a rafting trip down the Colorado River in 1986. It turned out to be not the kind of trip that Hatch—a former bishop—would have taken with the Mutual. His friend from the Senate had "an uncontrollable urge to do what has been done in rivers from time immemorial—go skinny-dipping," said Senator Hatch. "Several times, in fact."

But Senator Hatch got the last laugh. At the end of the trip he addressed a small gathering. He talked about the sights he'd seen on the raft trip, "sights I had never seen before!" he said.

Hatch's well-tanned Senate colleague roared.

WHEN ANN EDWARDS CANNON, the daughter of BYU's football coach LaVell Edwards, was earning high grades in Brigham Young University's English department, LaVell asked his daughter if she would tell her professors she was the daughter of the football coach.

Ann was shocked. "Dad," she said, "I don't want to win points that way."

"You?" said LaVell. "I wasn't talking about you. I'm the one who needs to earn points. We football players can stand some good publicity in the English department!"

THE PRAYER OF SERENITY often quoted at Alcoholics Anonymous meetings reads:

God grant me the serenity to accept the
     things I cannot change,
The courage to change the things I can,
And the wisdom to know the difference.

This sentiment is reflected in the story of a gardener whose yard was spotted by dandelions. He tried everything he knew to kill them—weeding, spraying, all kinds of chemicals—but was continually frustrated by their persistence. Finally he wrote the U.S. Department of Agriculture, listed the efforts he'd made, and asked what they advised him to do.

"We suggest," said a short reply, "you learn to love them."

THINK PEER PRESSURE IS TOUGH? Try mob pressure.

Or better yet, try courage. In 1839, Lyman Wight was imprisoned by an anti-Mormon militia, then confronted by its leader. "We do not wish to hurt you nor kill you," said the man to Brother Wight, "but we have one thing against you, and that is, you are too friendly to Joe Smith."

The mob leader asked Brother Wight to denounce the prophet. Brother Wight's response was that Joseph was the kindest, purest, most principled man he knew.

"I regret to tell you your doom is fixed," said the military leader. "You are sentenced to be shot tomorrow morning on the public square in Far West at eight o'clock."

"Shoot," responded Brother Wight, "and be damned."

The sentence was lifted the next morning; Brother Wight lived to stand up again for the things he believed in.

IF YOU'RE LOOKING FOR A word that describes the Word of Wisdom, try *wise*.

Take a lesson from the man who said, "I don't believe smoking is bad for you. I've smoked two packs of cigarettes a day since I was fourteen, and there's nothing wrong with my lung."

ABRAHAM LINCOLN UNDERSTOOD the Lord's admonition to love your enemies, to bless them that curse you, to do good to them that hate you. In a speech during the dark days of the Civil War, he spoke of the people of America's South as mistaken brothers and sisters, not as enemies to be exterminated. After his speech, a woman who was a strong Union partisan criticized his use of soft words. He shouldn't be consoling his enemies, she told Lincoln; he should be destroying them.

"Why, madam," said the president, "do I not destroy my enemies when I make them my friends?"

IF EVER YOU THINK THE WORLD revolves around you, remember a lesson taught by Camilla Eyring Kimball, the wife of Spencer W. Kimball. "It is good for one to be reminded that she is not indispensable," she said.

On a winter Sunday in 1972, not long before she was scheduled to teach a Relief Society lesson in her home ward, Sister Kimball entered the hospital with a perforated appendix. She alerted her Relief Society president, the president found a replacement, the lesson was taught, and life went on.

Life went on almost too well, in fact. The sisters in the ward gave high praise to the replacement teacher, Sister Kimball said. "I didn't get one bit of consolation that I was missed at all. The world has gone smoothly on its way with no concern that I haven't been on the job."

IN THE 1860S, CLARISSA YOUNG was a student in a Salt Lake City school—but she wasn't the teacher's pet. One day her teacher told her to sit in a corner of the schoolroom for misbehaving. Clarissa refused and went home instead—where she ran into her father, Brigham Young.

She reported what had happened at school. "Well," said the prophet when she concluded, "you can go and sit in a corner here."

THE WORTH OF SOULS IS GREAT in the sight
of the Lord, but in the sight of some of the
rest of us, that worth can be inadvertently dis-
counted.

Partway through a long vacation, a large
family stopped at a roadside restaurant. When
the waitress asked the family's eleven-year-old
son for his order, he looked to his mother for
instruction, but she was uncharacteristically
silent. "I'll have a hot dog!" the boy said.

The mother quickly vetoed the order.
"No," she said. "He'll have what the rest of us
are having."

But the waitress didn't seem to hear the
mother's mandate. "What would you like on
the hot dog?" she asked the boy.

The boy looked uncomfortable, glanced
at his mother, but then ventured, "I'd like
mustard, ketchup, pickles, and onions." After
the waitress wrote down his order and disap-
peared toward the kitchen, the young man
was incredulous. "She thinks I'm real!"

HUGH B. BROWN ADVISED the Saints to always keep a sense of humor—and he practiced what he preached. During his service in the Canadian army during World War I, he'd been overseas about a month when he received word that his wife had given birth to their fourth daughter.

His return message: "Don't have any more until I get home."

But humor is usually a matter of perspective. His wife, Elder Brown reported, "never did quite appreciate my comment."

C HOOSE YOU THIS DAY whom ye will serve," says Joshua. And remember: Not choosing—not making a decision—is a choice.

The plague of indecision is illustrated by the story of a group of kids who'd been missing since Halloween. They were finally discovered at the home of a chronically indecisive man. They had yelled, "Trick or treat!" and they'd been there, waiting for a decision, ever since.

WHEN A THEATER OPENED in Salt Lake City in the 1860s—with the strong encouragement of Brigham Young—enthusiastic patrons bought tickets with money, sausage, honey, chickens, and more. One person paid for his ticket with a turkey—and was given two spring chickens in change.

The only hard-and-fast rule regarding ticket purchases was posted on the theater programs: "Babies in arms, ten dollars each." The strategy worked. "I never heard of the ten dollars being paid," said one of Brigham's daughters.

O BE WISE," SAYS JACOB in the Book of Mormon.

And sometimes the best way to show your wisdom: O be quiet.

That thought is illustrated in the story of two brothers who went on a fishing trip. They rented all the equipment: the reels, the rods, the wading suits, the rowboat, the car, and even a cabin in the woods near the best fishing spot in the state. They spent a fortune. But the first day they went fishing they didn't catch anything. The same thing happened the next day; the same thing happened again the third day. Finally, on the last day of their vacation, one of the brothers caught a fish.

The drive home was really depressing. After eighty or ninety miles of silence, one brother turned to the other and said, "Do you realize this one lousy fish we caught cost us fifteen hundred dollars?"

"Wow," said the other brother. "It's a good thing we didn't catch any more!"

REMEMBER THE ADVICE IN Doctrine and Covenants, section ten: "Do not run faster or labor more than you have strength." Don't be like the man who was feeling a little run-down and made an appointment with his doctor. After examining him, the doctor told him his problem seemed to be that he was burning the candle at both ends.

"Well, I knew that before I came," said the man. "What I want from you is more wax."

P RIDE GOETH BEFORE DESTRUCTION," warns Proverbs. The point is illustrated with a story about a ship's captain who saw what looked like the light of another ship coming directly toward his vessel. He signaled the other ship, "Change your course ten degrees south." But the other ship failed to turn. It signaled, "Change *your* course ten degrees north."

The captain replied with some indignation, "I am a *captain*. Change *your* course south." The response was infuriating. It said, "Well, I am a seaman first class. Change *your* course north."

"I say change *your* course south," replied the captain. "I am on a battleship!"

"And I say change *your* course north," came the response. "I am in the lighthouse."

IN 1961, VICTOR L. BROWN received a telephone call in his Chicago home. The caller asked if he was planning on coming to general conference, which started the next day. "No," said Brother Brown. The man then asked if Brother Brown could come; Brother Brown said yes, he supposed so.

"The president of the Church would like to see you tomorrow morning at eight o'clock in his office," said the caller.

"Now have a good night's sleep," he added, "because it will be your last."

CAMILLA EYRING KIMBALL accompanied her husband, Spencer, to several area conferences in 1976. On their way to New Zealand, both of the Kimballs were sick, but as their plane neared its destination they felt better. They started to prepare themselves to assume their duties, which would start immediately after their plane touched down.

President Kimball, who had been sleeping, buttoned the top button of his shirt, straightened his tie, and asked his wife to brush his hair. He found that jet lag and sickness hadn't slowed her wit. "Which one?" she said.

NEVER GIVE UP ON A YOUNG PERSON. Be like the teacher who helped a small boy put on his galoshes one day after school. The galoshes seemed too small for the boy; they seemed almost smaller than his shoes. Still, the teacher tugged and stretched the boot until it finally squeaked onto the boy's foot. The other boot required a similar effort, but the teacher persisted until it, too, was snugly in place.

When she was done, the boy said, "These are not my galoshes." The disheveled teacher didn't lose heart. She knelt down again and with great effort, pulled the galoshes back off her student's feet.

"They are my sister's," the boy said when she was done, "but my mother made me wear them."

"No MATTER WHAT A MAN IS thought of by his fellowmen, if he is true, God is his friend, and he is rich indeed," said David O. McKay.

The problem is, not everyone is interested in the same kind of riches. An old widow visited a lawyer recently, and as she left his office, she asked if she could pay her bill in cash. The lawyer said, "Well, it's not a common practice, but sure." The bill totaled $100, so the woman opened her purse and took out a crisp new $100 bill and gave it to him.

Then, after the door had closed behind her, the lawyer noticed she had accidentally given him two bills, stuck together; she'd actually given him $200.

So he was faced with a serious ethical question: Should he tell his partner?

EARLY IN THE TWENTIETH CENTURY, Willard Bean, a former boxer, spent twenty-five years on a mission with his family in Palmyra, New York. One day he walked past a man who was watering his garden with a hose. "I understand you believe in baptism by immersion," said the man antagonistically. Elder Bean jumped the man's fence and stood next to him with his fists cocked. "Yes," he replied. "And we also believe in the laying on of hands."

Discouraged? Worn out? Relax. Things could be worse. You could be one of the early settlers of Manti, Utah, who endured severe winters, poor soil, rattlesnake invasions, Indian threats—and a very consistent diet. One pioneer shared what might have been a Sanpete County dinnertime theme song:

> Rabbits young and rabbits old,
> Rabbits hot and rabbits cold,
> Rabbits tender and rabbits tough,
> Thank the Lord, we've had rabbits enough.

KATHLEEN FOX AND HER FAMILY tried using formal court procedures to settle everyday family disputes. The idea: Give mom a break in her constant work as judge and jury. Case number one was Niki vs. Adam, in which Adam was charged with taking a dog away from his sister. Niki was asked to explain the details of the case, but in the best tradition of Perry Mason, her statement shocked the court. "I don't remember," she said.

Brother Fox, who was serving as judge, banged his gavel. "Case dismissed," he said. "Lack of evidence."

Amid giggles—and some sincere pleadings—the Foxes' system produced its intended results. It was, said Sister Fox, "the beginning of more peace."

Don't fall victim to the "if only" syndrome. We'd do things as a family *if only* we had more money. I'd read the scriptures every day *if only* I had more time.

Home economist and *Deseret News* food editor Winnifred Jardine worked at one time as a scout for a national women's magazine, searching for home and family improvement ideas that could be developed into magazine articles. "Without exception," said Sister Jardine, "the exciting and creative ideas were found in homes where money and space were limited and where the creativity of the owners was put to the test."

HUGH B. BROWN SUFFERED from a condition that caused chronic pain for almost fifty years—but he always maintained a sense of humor. One of the poems he quoted reads:

> My bifocals are wonderful
> My hearing aid's a find
> My dentures come in handy
> But how I miss my mind!

"LAY NOT UP FOR YOURSELVES treasures upon earth, where moth and rust doth corrupt, and where thieves break through and steal," said the Lord. "But lay up for yourselves treasures in heaven."

An apocryphal story of a wealthy man's death illustrates the point. Two of the man's friends stood before the casket. "How much property did he leave?" asked one.

"He left all of it," said the other.

IN A 1971 CONFERENCE TALK on the reality of Satan, Marion G. Romney related the story of a young woman who decided she couldn't marry her boyfriend because of differences in their beliefs.

"He does not believe in the devil," she told her mother.

"Go ahead and marry him," her mother replied. "You and I will change his mind."

YOU KNOW THE OLD SAYINGS: "Lighten up." "Look on the bright side." "When life hands you lemons, make lemonade." And when life hands you molasses?

Joe Bischoff was a farmer in central Utah in the early 1900s who hired out to another man for a summer's worth of work. But by the end of the summer, he found his boss wasn't much wealthier than he was. Brother Bischoff's pay for his three months of work: a barrel of molasses.

His response wasn't to hire a lawyer. He looked on the bright side. By Christmas the molasses was entirely gone. "And we had," said Joe, "the five sweetest kids in town."

Before JOHN R. LASATER became a General
Authority, he served as a member of an
American delegation that visited Morocco. The
delegation was transported through the
Moroccan desert in a procession of speeding
limousines, but the procession stopped when
one of the vehicles hit and injured a stray sheep
belonging to a local shepherd. Brother Lasater's
vehicle pulled up as the limousine's driver and
the shepherd were discussing Moroccan law.

"Because the king's vehicle has injured
one of the sheep belonging to the old shepherd, the shepherd is now entitled to one
hundred times its value at maturity," Elder
Lasater's interpreter explained. "However,
under the same law, the injured sheep must be
slain and the meat divided among the people."

The interpreter added: "But the old shepherd will not accept the money. They never do."

Elder Lasater asked why.

"Because of the love he has for each of his
sheep," said the interpreter.

WHEN N. ELDON TANNER and his family moved from a small, rural town in western Canada to Edmonton, Canada's large capital city, the Tanners' four young daughters learned much about the world. One discovery was the previously unheard-of thought that milk and bread came from stores. Helen Tanner, who was five at the time, was especially astonished. "I thought milk came from cows and bread came from the oven," she said.

ONE OF THE FEW WORDS that was not in J. Golden Kimball's vocabulary: *pride*.

"I am not accustomed to speaking to audiences out of doors," he said once. "I have always had them closed in where they could not get away."

On another occasion, he cited himself as a prime exhibit to prove the reality of revelation in the Church. "A lot of people in the Church believe that men are called to leadership in the Church by revelation, and some do not," he said. "But I'll tell you, when the Lord calls an old mule skinner like me to be a General Authority, there's got to be revelation."

OVER TWENTY YEARS AGO, Sterling W. Sill quoted a poem that teaches a lesson that's absolutely true today: We worry too much.

> Of all our troubles great and small,
> The greatest are those
> That never happen at all.

A story told by American hockey player Phil Esposito illustrates the point. Esposito and some teammates were in the Soviet Union in Moscow in the early 1970s. Fearing their hotel room might be bugged, they scoured the room for microphones. Their fears were confirmed when they found a suspicious look-ing metallic object embedded in the floor under a rug.

"We figured we had found the bug," said Esposito. "We dug it out of the floor. And we heard a crash beneath us. We had released the anchor to the chandelier in the ceiling below."

WHEN A MORMON CONVERT broke his spine in a mining accident in Wales in 1849, local doctors said the man would die within a matter of hours. Sympathetic onlookers were despondent, but the injured man kept his faith and called for the elders. William Howells was president of the local branch; he and his two counselors responded to the call. They administered to the man and, in the name of Jesus Christ, commanded him to stand.

"Those who stood around the bed heard the bones of the sick man's body crack as they slid back into their places," wrote Brother Howells's daughter, "and the man arose from his bed and gave thanks to God for his mercy."

Sin HAS MANY TOOLS," said Oliver Wendell Holmes, "but a lie is the handle which fits them all."

Marvin J. Ashton knew a man who created a tangled web of lies and deceit. "He suffered . . . the pains of a victim entrapped in his own snare," said the apostle. The man once told Elder Ashton: "I have been living lies for so long and have told so many over the years that, frankly, I don't really know when I am telling the truth."

"He who lives a lie," said Elder Ashton, "is the servant of the lie."

THOSE WHO ASSOCIATED with Joseph Fielding Smith soon learned there was another side to the apostle's scholarly and serious image. Once, Elder Smith came home from a conference in California with a sackful of fresh olives he'd picked, which he offered to a fellow Church leader. The unsuspecting brother had never bitten into a bitter green olive—and when he did, he puckered up so intensely it appeared the olive had just bitten him.

"What's the matter—did you get a bad one?" asked Elder Smith sweetly. "Here, you had better try another one."

· NOVEMBER 24 ·

IN JUNE OF 1834, FIVE ARMED MEN rode into a Mormon camp in Missouri and told the Saints they would "see hell before morning." A mob of men from three counties was gathering just down the river, the men said; their purpose was the total destruction of the Mormon camp.

But as the five men left the camp, a violent storm began to rage. The earth shook; hailstones knocked branches off trees; streams and rivers swelled and gushed; trees fell; lightning struck. One member of the mob was killed by lightning; another was injured by a frightened horse. The mob scattered.

Two days later the leader of the group strode into the Mormon camp. "I see there is an almighty power that protects this people," he said. "I started from Richmond, Ray County, with a company of armed men, having a fixed determination to destroy you, but was kept back by the storm."

OPENING THE MAIL ONE DAY, George Albert Smith and his secretary ran across a letter from a man interested in the Church's position on cocoa and cremation. Said President Smith: "Write and tell him they're both hot."

Iᴛ ɪs ɪᴍᴘᴏʀᴛᴀɴᴛ ᴛʜᴀᴛ ᴡᴇ ᴍᴀᴋᴇ ᴜᴘ our minds early in life as to what we will do and what we will not do," said N. Eldon Tanner. "Long before the moment of temptation comes we should have determined that we will resist."

Young Emily Nash provides an example. She was on her way to meet her mother's uncle. As they made the trip, her parents explained that he was a good man, not a member of the Church, and that he smoked.

Emily was only four, but her commitment was firm enough to make Nancy Reagan proud. "If Uncle Frank asks me to smoke," she said, "I will just say no!"

THE STORY IS TOLD OF AN OLDER FAN at a BYU football game whose seat was directly behind a young student who kept standing up to cheer. After some exasperation over his blocked view, he tapped the student on the shoulder. "Ma'am, excuse me, but could you sit down?" he asked. "You're blocking my vision."

"Oh, I'm sorry," she said. "I didn't know you were having one."

WHEN SPENCER W. KIMBALL was an apostle, he interviewed a missionary who had almost completed his mission and would soon return home. Elder Kimball asked the young man if he had any plans.

"Oh, I plan to go back to college," said the elder, "then I hope to fall in love and get married."

The missionary answered with a twinkle in his eye, but Elder Kimball's response was thoughtful and wise. "Well, don't just pray to marry the one you love," said the apostle. "Instead, pray to love the one you marry."

THE SCRIPTURES COUNSEL US to judge not unrighteously, and the best way to do that is to judge not at all. As evidence, consider the story of two judges at a state fair who couldn't decide which of two big bulls should receive a blue ribbon. After great discussion, they noticed a young boy watching the bulls, and decided to have him pick which bull should win the championship ribbon. The boy examined the bulls only briefly before picking the winner. After the ribbon was awarded, the judges asked the boy what prompted his decision.

"I just chose the one I thought would give the best milk," he said.

J. GOLDEN KIMBALL CONDEMNED what he called "halfway-men"—those who upheld their beliefs in public but ignored their commitments whenever they could get away with it. "They are like the dying man who was asked by his minister, 'Will you denounce the devil and his workings?'" said J. Golden in a talk. "The dying man looked up in a feeble and distressed way and said, 'Please don't ask me to do that. I am going to a strange country, and I don't want to make any enemies.'"

WHEN N. ELDON TANNER was thirty, he served as second counselor in the Cardston Canada First Ward, where he worked with the Scouts and deacons—many of whom weren't coming to church. The problem was that few boys had Sunday clothes. So Eldon struck a deal: If the boys would come to church in their coveralls, the young counselor would, too.

To young N. Eldon Tanner, wrote a biographer, "principle was absolute, but fashion was negotiable."

The result: One hundred percent attendance in the ward's three quorums of deacons.

THE SPIRIT OF THE GOSPEL is optimistic; it trusts in God and looks on the bright side of things," said Orson F. Whitney in 1917. That spirit is reflected in a story told by Bryant S. Hinckley, the father of Gordon B. Hinckley, about a man who fell off the roof of a seventeen-story building. As he passed the seventh floor, he was heard to say, "Okay so far."

WHEN HAROLD B. LEE WAS PRESIDENT of the Church, a Church film crew tried to prod him into wearing makeup for the filming of the prophet's Christmas message. But President Lee resisted, even though he looked wan and weary. "All important people have to wear makeup for filming," said the film's director. "President Eisenhower used to have makeup put on him and President Nixon has found he needs to wear it for television appearances."

"Yes," said President Lee with a smile, "but I'm not running for anything."

MATTHEW COWLEY LEARNED a great deal about faith in his work with the Polynesian people. He also learned that boys will be boys. Twelve years after he blessed a blind infant and gave the child both his name and his sight, Elder Cowley ran into the boy's branch president. "Brother Cowley, the worst thing you ever did was to bless that child to receive his vision," said the man. "He's the meanest kid in the neighborhood, always getting into mischief."

Elder Cowley's response? "I was thrilled," he said.

TRAIN UP A CHILD IN THE WAY he should go, and when he is old, he will not depart from it," says Proverbs.

But the child might get a little exasperated with you along the way. Marvin J. Ashton told the story of walking past the Salt Lake Temple with his nine-year-old grandson. Pointing to the temple, he asked, "What's that building, Jeff?"

"He gave me one of those looks that only a nine-year-old can give you when you have asked a five-year-old question," said Elder Ashton. "It's the temple," said the boy. The apostle asked another question: "What are temples for?"

"It's where I'm going to get married someday," said Jeff.

"Thank God," said Elder Ashton, "for caring parents who teach their children early in their lives to look forward to the temple!"

AN EARLY LATTER-DAY SAINT once shared with Joseph Smith his theory—which he explained in flowery detail—that all of eternity was filled with the Spirit of God. Asking for Joseph's opinion, the Prophet answered that the idea seemed beautiful, and he could find only one fault with it.

"What is that?" asked the man.

"It is not true," said the Prophet.

WHEN LEGRAND RICHARDS was a young man, he joined some acquaintances for a dance at Saltair, the fabled resort on the shores of the Great Salt Lake. Partway through the evening, a young woman invited LeGrand to join her and her friends at dinner. The two clasped hands and walked together downstairs to where their private table was waiting—until LeGrand saw that a bottle of beer had been set by each plate.

"What's the matter?" asked the young woman. "Are you too good to drink a little beer?"

"I guess I am," he said before making a fast exit, "and I thought you were, too."

EVEN IN HIS LATER YEARS, Henry B. Eyring—a renowned scientist and the father of the apostle—retained his energy and enthusiasm. Well past age sixty, he'd jump from the floor in the university classrooms where he lectured to the top of his desk, and he challenged his students to races.

Brother Eyring made no unnecessary concessions to his physical limitations. One day he ran into Spencer W. Kimball in the Church Administration Building. President Kimball was surprised to see his spirited and vigorous friend—who was also his brother-in-law—leaning on a cane.

"Henry," said the prophet, "what is the cane for?"

Answered Brother Eyring: "Style, President, style."

RANDY BACHMAN WAS A DRUMMER in the Guess Who—a popular rock and roll band in Canada—before he met a Mormon girl and joined the Church. His life was changed one night in a Canadian café. His future wife and her girlfriend walked into the café—and Randy knew right away there was something different about them. How different, he didn't know.

"We thought they looked very California," he said. "It turned out they were very Salt Lake."

Ezra Taft Benson told the story of an enthusiastic young insurance salesman, fresh out of college, who was bound and determined to sell insurance to everyone he met. He walked into a farmyard one autumn morning with a bounce in his step and fire in his eyes—and met an old farmer, his back bent by years of labor, standing near a field of grain.

"Look up, my good man, there's much to live for!" said the salesman, noticing the old man's hunched back and slouched shoulders.

The farmer responded by asking the young salesman to look out at the field of wheat. "Do you notice that some of the heads are bent over?" asked the farmer.

"Yes," said the salesman.

"Those are the ones," said the farmer, "with the grain in them."

WHEN LEGRAND RICHARDS was presiding bishop, he attended a meeting in the Salt Lake Temple with all of the Church's general authorities. Serious issues were raised and addressed, and after a lengthy dialogue, Bishop Richards shared a thought that struck his colleagues as wise—and true.

"Now, brethren," said Bishop Richards, "I understand all that we discussed, but until the bishops move, nothing will happen. Everything above the bishop is all talk."

REMEMBER THIS NEXT TIME you speak in church.

"Wise is the man who says what needs to be said, but not all that could be said," said Marvin J. Ashton in 1976. Take a lesson from Calvin Coolidge, the famously reticent president who earned the nickname "Silent Cal." After church one Sunday, President Coolidge had a visitor who asked him what topic the pastor preached about.

"Sin," said Coolidge.

"What did he say about sin?" asked the visitor.

Coolidge's famous response: "He was against it."

PART OF MANAGING YOUR MONEY wisely is knowing when to spend it. Don't be like the father who bragged that he took his family out for cookies and juice for the first time recently. "They really enjoyed it," he said. "They'd never given blood before."

· DECEMBER 14 ·

WRITER ELBERT HUBBARD often shared his opinion on issues of the day in a manner that incited strong opposition. But in responding to that criticism, Hubbard often turned his enemies into friends. When someone wrote to criticize one of his essays, Hubbard usually sent a reply like this:

"Come to think it over, I don't entirely agree with it myself. Not everything I wrote yesterday appeals to me today. I am glad to learn what you think on the subject. The next time you are in the neighborhood you must visit us, and we'll get this subject threshed out for all time. So here is a handclasp over the miles, and I am

"Yours sincerely."

Hubbard learned the Old Testament's advice: "A soft answer turneth away wrath."

PARENTS: IF YOU EVER WONDER whether or not you have an influence on your children, remember the story of a father who took his three young sons on a summertime trip to Yellowstone Park. Upon their return, they dropped by Grandma's to report their adventures. And the first thing out of their mouths? They didn't describe the bears, geysers, elk, moose, hot pots, mountains, fish, rivers, or lakes. "Grandma!" they said, "Daddy got a ticket for speeding!"

BRIGHAM YOUNG ONCE PASSED along the medical opinion of a New York physician who said that snuff had no harmful effects on the brain. "There is no fear of snuff's hurting the brain of anyone," Brother Brigham reported, "for no person that has brains will take snuff."

SET A BUDGET, said N. Eldon Tanner, and stick to it. "Many think a budget robs them of their freedom," he said in a conference talk. "On the contrary, successful people have learned that a budget makes real economic freedom possible."

He illustrated the point by referring to a telegram sent by a young man in college to his father. "No mon, no fun, your son," wired the boy.

The father's response is often worth emulating, President Tanner said. He wired back: "How sad, too bad, your dad."

AN ALERT PROOFREADER prevented a Church resource manual, *Teaching: No Greater Call,* from being incorrectly listed in a Church catalog, said Ardeth G. Kapp. The mistake would have been a minor typographical error but a major philosophical one. The original listing: *Teaching: No Great Call.*

Matthew Cowley was counseled by George Albert Smith to avoid writing his sermons in advance and instead to let the Lord guide him in what he would say. Before one sermon, Elder Cowley said he felt like the minister who stood up to preach without adequate notes. Said the minister: "Brothers and sisters, I have not had any time during the week to prepare my sermon because of my social obligations, so I will just have to stand up and let the Lord speak through me. But next week I will promise to do better."

JOSEPH FIELDING SMITH HONORED his parents. He also respected the talents of his father's mare, Juney, who used her teeth to unlock gates and unfasten straps and buckles. Joseph F. Smith charged his son to keep Juney in her corral, but whenever the horse escaped, Joseph Fielding recalled, "Father said to me, half humorously, that Juney seemed to be smarter than I was."

After one escape, the elder Smith secured the horse in her corral, but as soon as he and his son walked away, the horse came trotting after them. "I could not refrain from suggesting to Father," said Joseph Fielding, "that I was not the only one whose head compared unfavorably with the mare's."

IN A LANDMARK ADDRESS entitled "Constancy Amid Change," N. Eldon Tanner told the story of an immigrant businessman who managed his affairs very simply, with his cash in his cash register and his receipts in a shoebox.

"I don't see how you can run your business this way," said the man's well-educated son. "How do you know what your profit is?"

"Son," the father answered, "when I got off the boat, I had only the pants I was wearing. Today your sister is an art teacher, your brother is a doctor, and you're an accountant. I have a car, a home, and a good business. Everything is paid for. So you add it all up, subtract the pants, and there's my profit."

JAMES E. TALMAGE WAS AN unrepentant workaholic, despite the best efforts of his colleagues to reform him. Heber J. Grant eventually persuaded him to take up golf and said he should stick to it until he hit "a real golf shot," after which the prophet would stop exhorting him to lighten his workload. The studious apostle reluctantly agreed. One day he endured a short lesson on a golfer's stance and swing, then hit a long, straight shot that flew 200 yards toward the hole. It was clearly a real shot; the prophet was impressed.

"If I have carried out my part of the agreement, then I shall call on you to live up to yours," stated Elder Talmage. "I should like to get back to the office, where I have a great deal of work waiting."

A MORMON FAMILY had seven young children and just one car. The father, a new dentist, often took the car to his office, so when the mother wanted to go anywhere, she and the kids took the bus.

When the bus stopped for the woman and her children one day, the mother climbed up the stairs and dropped a token in the slot for herself and seven more for each of her children. As they all entered the bus and marched up the aisle, the bus driver was dumbfounded. "Lady, are these all your children, or is this a picnic?" he said.

"They are all my children," said the mother, "and it's no picnic!"

WHEN APOSTLE ORSON F. WHITNEY was a bishop, one of the children in his ward told his mother the story of the miracle of the loaves and the fishes, which had been the subject of that day's Primary lesson. The boy's mother asked how many people had been fed. "Five thousand," said the boy. And what did Jesus feed them with? "Five loaves of bread and two fishes," he said. "How is that possible?" she asked. "Well," said the boy, "I don't believe those in the middle got any."

ONE CHRISTMAS, ELAINE L. JACK decided to be both creative and economical. She decided to flock her Christmas tree herself.

"I was sure I could create a beautiful tree for much less than a tree cost on the lot," she said. With a home flocking kit, a water bottle, and a vacuum cleaner, she started the job.

"It worked!" said Sister Jack. "Synthetic snow made the tree look like a winter wonderland."

But the wonder was fleeting. "As I finished and stepped back to admire my Currier-and-Ives tree," she said, "I noticed that the wall, the sofa, the piano, and the chairs were also part of my winter wonderland."

"Snow removal that year continued into June," said Sister Jack.

WHEN TWO PRESCHOOLERS FOUGHT over a doll, their mother lost her temper and settled the argument by throwing the doll out the window. She then delivered a short lecture on sharing.

But what we do always overshadows what we say. Later that day the mother found the children throwing loaves of bread out the window.

Eight armed and angry men stormed into Lucy Mack Smith's house one day, looking to kill her son Joseph and all his followers. "I suppose you intend to kill me, with the rest?" asked Sister Smith.

"Yes, we do," said the ruffian.

"Very well," said the mother of the prophet. "I want you to act like gentlemen about it, and do the job quick. Just shoot me down at once, then I shall be at rest, but I should not like to be murdered by inches."

"There it is again," answered the hoodlum. "You tell a Mormon that you will kill him, and they will always tell you, 'That is nothing—if you kill us, we shall be happy.'"

No one died in the Smith house that day.

DAVID O. MCKAY WAS FOURTEEN when he
received a patriarchal blessing that said, in
part, "It shall be thy lot to sit in council with
thy brethren and preside among the people
and exhort the Saints to faithfulness." After
the blessing, the future prophet's father, who
was a bishop at the time, put his hands on his
son's shoulders and said, "My boy, you have
something to do besides playing marbles."

But young David was less moved by the
blessing than his father was. He walked into
the next room and told his mother, "If he
thinks I'm going to stop playing marbles, he
is mistaken."

ALMA HEATON TELLS THE STORY about when Mark Twain visited Utah and got involved in a discussion with a local brother about the question of polygamy. After a long and fruitless debate, the Mormon asked the author if he could quote a single passage of scripture that forbade polygamy.

"Certainly!" said Twain. "'No man can serve two masters.'"

SERVICE IS THE GREAT ANTIDOTE to loneliness. Take the example of eighty-seven-year-old Amy Gent, who was never lonely, even though she was the only member of the Church in her family and had been widowed two times. "She read the scriptures every day," explained her home teacher. "Once she asked me to bring her some missionary tracts, which I thought were to vary her reading. I gave them to her saying, 'You will enjoy reading these, Sister Gent.' 'Oh, they are not for me,' she answered. 'I visit an old lady, and I want to share the gospel with her.'"

MARION G. ROMNEY TOLD THE STORY of an old grandfather he knew, a good member of the Church, who had a well-deserved reputation for going on too long whenever he gave a talk. After a while the leaders of the old brother's ward thought they needed to give him a speaking assignment, so they asked him to stand and share his advice on what people could do to live as long he had lived and still serve in the Lord's kingdom.

The result was the shortest sermon of the old man's life.

"Keep breathing," he said.

· Sources ·

Jan 1: Ardeth Greene Kapp, *My Neighbor, My Sister, My Friend* (Salt Lake City: Deseret Book, 1990), 91.

Jan 2: Matthew Cowley, *Matthew Cowley Speaks* (Salt Lake City: Deseret Book, 1976), 344.

Jan 3: Max Nolan, "J. Golden Kimball in the South," *New Era,* July 1985, 8.

Jan 4: Richard S. Van Wagoner and Steven C. Walker, *A Book of Mormons* (Salt Lake City: Signature, 1982), 46.

Jan 5: Personal records of the author.

Jan 6: Orson F. Whitney, general conference address, April 4, 1926; reprinted in *Conference Report,* 34.

Jan 7: D. Arthur Haycock and Heidi S. Swinton, *In the Company of Prophets* (Salt Lake City: Deseret Book, 1993), 41.

Jan 8: "Associate Remembers Good Times, Quick Wit of Dear Friend, Neighbor," *Church News,* March 11, 1995, 19.

Jan 9: Emerson Roy West, *Profiles of the Presidents* (Salt Lake City: Deseret Book, 1980), 73.

Jan 10: Richard L. Evans Jr., *Richard L. Evans: The Man and His Message* (Salt Lake City: Bookcraft, 1973), 14.

Jan 11: Edward L. Kimball and Andrew E. Kimball Jr., *Spencer W. Kimball* (Salt Lake City: Bookcraft, 1977), 420.

Jan 12: Emerson Roy West, *Profiles of the Presidents* (Salt Lake City: Deseret Book, 1980), 250.

Jan 13: Thomas E. Cheney, *The Golden Legacy* (Layton: Peregrine Smith, 1974), 81.

Jan 14: Salt Lake Parleys Stake conference, January 28, 1995.

Jan 15: *The Time of Your Life: Selections from the New Era Magazine* (Salt Lake City: Bookcraft, 1977), 86–87.

Jan 16: Glen L. Rudd, general conference address, April 2, 1988; reprinted in the *Ensign*, May 1988, 28.

Jan 17: G. Homer Durham, *N. Eldon Tanner: His Life and Service* (Salt Lake City: Deseret Book, 1982), 171–72.

Jan 18: D. Arthur Haycock and Heidi S. Swinton, *In the Company of Prophets* (Salt Lake City: Deseret Book, 1993), 33.

Jan 19: D. Arthur Haycock and Heidi S. Swinton, *In the Company of Prophets* (Salt Lake City: Deseret Book, 1993), 62.

Jan 20: Salt Lake Parleys Stake conference, January 28, 1995.

Jan 21: D. Arthur Haycock and Heidi S. Swinton, *In the Company of Prophets* (Salt Lake City: Deseret Book, 1993), 63.

Jan 22: Leon R. Hartshorn, *Classic Stories from the Lives of Our Prophets* (Salt Lake City: Deseret Book, 1988), 204.

Jan 23: Sheri L. Dew, *Sharlene Wells, Miss America* (Salt Lake City: Deseret Book, 1985), 101.

Jan 24: Joseph F. McConkie, *True and Faithful* (Salt Lake City: Bookcraft, 1971), 74.

Jan 25: Edward L. Kimball and Andrew E. Kimball Jr., *Spencer W. Kimball* (Salt Lake City: Bookcraft, 1977), 282.

Jan 26: Excerpts from October general conference, *New Era,* January 1973, 22.

Jan 27: *The Time of Your Life: Selections from the New Era Magazine* (Salt Lake City: Bookcraft, 1977), 109–110.

Jan 28: *The Life of Joseph Fielding Smith* (Salt Lake City: Deseret Book, 1972), 49.

Jan 29: Personal records of the author.

Jan 30: Personal records of the author.

Jan 31: *The Time of Your Life: Selections from the New Era Magazine* (Salt Lake City: Bookcraft, 1977), 108.

Feb 1: Personal records of the author.

Feb 2: Emerson Roy West, *Profiles of the Presidents* (Salt Lake City: Deseret Book, 1980), 219.

Feb 3: Lucy Gertsch Thomson, *Stories That Live* (Salt Lake City: Deseret Book, 1956), 46–47.

Feb 4: Joe J. Christensen, general conference address, October 2, 1993; reprinted in *Ensign,* November 1993, 12.

Feb 5: Leonard J. Arrington and Susan Arrington Madsen, *Sunbonnet Sisters* (Salt Lake City: Bookcraft, 1984), 4.

Feb 6: Stephen L Richards, "The Responsibility of Relief Society Members to Their Home and the Priesthood," Relief Society magazine, December 1951, 796.

Feb 7: Davida Dalton, "In His Mother's Footsteps," *Ensign,* April 1994, 11.

Feb 8: David O. McKay, address to the general conference of the Relief Society, October 1, 1953; reprinted in Relief Society magazine, December 1953, 790.

Feb 9: Llewelyn R. McKay, *Home Memories of President David O. McKay* (Salt Lake City: Deseret Book, 1959), 41, 109–110.

Feb 10: Russell M. Nelson, general conference address, April 3, 1993; reprinted in *Ensign,* May 1993, 39.

Feb 11: Leon R. Hartshorn, *Outstanding Stories by General Authorities* (Salt Lake City: Deseret Book, 1970), 199.

Feb 12: Ardeth Greene Kapp, *My Neighbor, My Sister, My Friend* (Salt Lake City: Deseret Book, 1990), 177.

· Sources ·

Feb 13: Leonard J. Arrington and Susan Arrington Madsen, *Sunbonnet Sisters* (Salt Lake City: Bookcraft, 1984), 4.

Feb 14: David O. McKay, address to employees of the Physical Facilities Department of the Church, Hotel Utah, 1965 (as quoted in *LDS Speakers Sourcebook,* Aspen Press, 1991, 460).

Feb 15: Leon R. Hartshorn, *Classic Stories from the Lives of Our Prophets* (Salt Lake City: Deseret Book, 1975), 257.

Feb 16: Edward L. Kimball and Andrew E. Kimball Jr., *Spencer W. Kimball* (Salt Lake City: Bookcraft, 1977), 232.

Feb 17: Llewelyn R. McKay, *Home Memories of President David O. McKay* (Salt Lake City: Deseret Book, 1959), 63.

Feb 18: D. Arthur Haycock and Heidi S. Swinton, *In the Company of Prophets* (Salt Lake City: Deseret Book, 1993), 59.

Feb 19: Edward L. Kimball and Andrew E. Kimball Jr., *Spencer W. Kimball* (Salt Lake City: Bookcraft, 1977), 414.

Feb 20: Clarissa Young Spencer, *Brigham Young at Home* (Salt Lake City: Deseret Book, 1972), 160.

Feb 21: Thomas E. Cheney, *The Golden Legacy* (Layton: Peregrine Smith, 1974), 129.

· SOURCES ·

Feb 22: Emerson Roy West, *Profiles of the Presidents* (Salt Lake City: Deseret Book, 1980), 300.

Feb 23: Edward L. Kimball and Andrew E. Kimball Jr., *Spencer W. Kimball* (Salt Lake City: Bookcraft, 1977), 309.

Feb 24: Hugh B. Brown, *An Abundant Life: The Memoirs of Hugh B. Brown* (Salt Lake City: Signature, 1988), 13.

Feb 25: Bryant S. Hinckley, *That Ye Might Have Joy* (Salt Lake City: Bookcraft, 1958), 30.

Feb 26: Hugh B. Brown, *An Abundant Life: The Memoirs of Hugh B. Brown* (Salt Lake City: Signature, 1988), 108.

Feb 27: Emerson Roy West, *Profiles of the Presidents* (Salt Lake City: Deseret Book, 1980), 73.

Feb 28: Thomas E. Cheney, *The Golden Legacy* (Layton: Peregrine Smith, 1974), 51.

Mar 1: Leon R. Hartshorn, *Exceptional Stories from the Lives of Our Apostles* (Salt Lake City: Deseret Book, 1972), 194.

Mar 2: *The Time of Your Life: Selections from the New Era Magazine* (Salt Lake City: Bookcraft, 1977), 116–17.

Mar 3: LaVell Edwards with Lee Benson, *LaVell: Airing It Out* (Salt Lake City: Shadow Mountain, 1995), 185.

Mar 4: Kimball, Smith, Ashton, et al., *Joy* (Salt Lake City: Deseret Book, 1980), 31.

Mar 5: Excerpts from October general conference, *New Era,* January 1973, 22.

Mar 6: Kimball, Smith, Ashton, et al., *Joy* (Salt Lake City: Deseret Book, 1980), 82.

Mar 7: Sheri L. Dew, *Sharlene Wells, Miss America* (Salt Lake City: Deseret Book, 1985), 61.

Mar 8: Kimball, Smith, Ashton, et al., *Joy* (Salt Lake City: Deseret Book, 1980), 124.

Mar 9: Ardeth Greene Kapp, "Taking Upon Us His Name," *New Era,* April 1982, 44.

Mar 10: Jeanette McKay Morrell, *Highlights in the Life of President David O. McKay* (Salt Lake City: Deseret Book, 1966), 42.

Mar 11: Michaelene P. Grassli, general women's meeting address, September 26, 1992; reprinted in *Ensign,* November 1992, 94.

Mar 12: Marvin J. Ashton, *Ye Are My Friends* (Salt Lake City: Deseret Book, 1982), 89–90.

Mar 13: Leon R. Hartshorn, *Classic Stories from the Lives of Our Prophets* (Salt Lake City: Deseret Book, 1975), 17.

Mar 14: Thomas E. Cheney, *The Golden Legacy* (Layton: Peregrine Smith, 1974), 44.

Mar 15: Marvin J. Ashton, *Ye Are My Friends* (Salt Lake City: Deseret Book, 1982), 143.

Mar 16: Personal records of the author.

· SOURCES ·

Mar 17: Ardeth Greene Kapp, *My Neighbor, My Sister, My Friend* (Salt Lake City: Deseret Book, 1990), 85–86.

Mar 18: *The Time of Your Life: Selections from the New Era Magazine* (Salt Lake City: Bookcraft, 1977), 116.

Mar 19: Clarissa Young Spencer, *Brigham Young at Home* (Salt Lake City: Deseret Book, 1972), 164.

Mar 20: Matthew Cowley, *Matthew Cowley Speaks* (Salt Lake City: Deseret Book, 1976), 2.

Mar 21: Ardeth Greene Kapp, *My Neighbor, My Sister, My Friend* (Salt Lake City: Deseret Book, 1990), 165.

Mar 22: D. Arthur Haycock and Heidi S. Swinton, *In the Company of Prophets* (Salt Lake City: Deseret Book, 1993), 73.

Mar 23: *This People,* December 1987, 63.

Mar 24: Thomas E. Cheney, *The Golden Legacy* (Layton: Peregrine Smith, 1974), 9.

Mar 25: Personal records of the author.

Mar 26: Marcia Stornetta, "Grandma's Legacy," *Ensign,* June 1994, 62.

Mar 27: Leon R. Hartshorn, *Classic Stories from the Lives of Our Prophets* (Salt Lake City: Deseret Book, 1988), 361.

Mar 28: "Young Women Fireside 1981," *New Era,* July 1981, 17.

· SOURCES ·

Mar 29: *This People*, April 1985, 33–34.

Mar 30: Personal records of the author.

Mar 31: Emerson Roy West, *Profiles of the Presidents* (Salt Lake City: Deseret Book, 1980), 229.

Apr 1: Richard S. Van Wagoner and Steven C. Walker, *A Book of Mormons* (Salt Lake City: Signature, 1982), 109.

Apr 2: Thomas E. Cheney, *The Golden Legacy* (Layton: Peregrine Smith, 1974), 33.

Apr 3: Kimball, Tanner, Romney, et al., *Prayer* (Salt Lake City: Deseret Book, 1977), 43.

Apr 4: Ruth B. Wright, general conference address, April 3, 1994; reprinted in *Ensign*, May 1994, 84.

Apr 5: Matthew Cowley, *Matthew Cowley Speaks* (Salt Lake City: Deseret Book, 1976), 304.

Apr 6: Carol Cornwall Madsen and Susan Staker Oman, *Sisters and Little Saints: 100 Years of Primary* (Salt Lake City: Deseret Book, 1979), 130.

Apr 7: Stephen Webster, "This Is the Place," *Las Vegas Latter-day Family Journal*, September 21, 1988, 2.

Apr 8: *Woman to Woman: Selected Talks from the BYU Women's Conferences* (Salt Lake City: Deseret Book, 1986), 16–17.

Apr 9: Clarissa Young Spencer, *Brigham Young at Home* (Salt Lake City: Deseret Book, 1972), 213.

Apr 10: Eleanor Knowles, *Howard W. Hunter* (Salt Lake City: Deseret Book, 1994), 233.

Apr 11: *Wisconsin State Journal,* February 3, 1996.

Apr 12: Thomas E. Cheney, *The Golden Legacy* (Layton: Peregrine Smith, 1974), 25.

Apr 13: Jeffrey R. and Patricia T. Holland, *On Earth as It Is in Heaven* (Salt Lake City: Deseret Book, 1989), 99.

Apr 14: Edward L. Kimball and Andrew E. Kimball Jr., *Spencer W. Kimball* (Salt Lake City: Bookcraft, 1977), 412.

Apr 15: Joe J. Christensen, "Resolutions" from "Speaking Today," *Ensign,* in December 1994, 65.

Apr 16: Edward L. Kimball and Andrew E. Kimball Jr., *Spencer W. Kimball* (Salt Lake City: Bookcraft, 1977), 333.

Apr 17: Ardeth Greene Kapp, *My Neighbor, My Sister, My Friend* (Salt Lake City: Deseret Book, 1990), 179.

Apr 18: G. Homer Durham, *N. Eldon Tanner: His Life and Service* (Salt Lake City: Deseret Book, 1982), 113.

Apr 19: Glen L. Rudd, general conference address, April 2, 1988; reprinted in *Ensign,* May 1988, 36.

Apr 20: Linda and Richard Eyre, *Teaching Your Children Values* (New York: Simon & Schuster, 1993), 190.

Apr 21: Personal records of the author.

Apr 22: Emerson Roy West, *Profiles of the Presidents* (Salt Lake City: Deseret Book, 1980), 229.

Apr 23: Matthew Cowley, *Matthew Cowley Speaks* (Salt Lake City: Deseret Book, 1976), 72.

Apr 24: J. Randolph Ayre, *Illustrations to Inspire* (Salt Lake City: Bookcraft, 1968), 50.

Apr 25: Leon R. Hartshorn, *Classic Stories from the Lives of Our Prophets* (Salt Lake City: Deseret Book, 1988), 203.

Apr 26: Dwan J. Young, general women's meeting address, September 28, 1985; reprinted in *Ensign,* November 1985, 92; Spencer W. Kimball quote in *Ensign,* December 1974, 5 (as quoted in *LDS Speakers Sourcebook,* Aspen Press, 1991, 432).

Apr 27: Leon R. Hartshorn, *Remarkable Stories from the Lives of Latter-day Saint Women* (Salt Lake City: Deseret Book, 1975), 179.

Apr 28: Address to Parleys Fifth Ward Relief Society, March 8, 1995.

· SOURCES ·

Apr 29: Rex D. Pinegar, "Grandfather Johansen's Example," *New Era*, September 1977, 4.

Apr 30: Leon R. Hartshorn, *Classic Stories from the Lives of Our Prophets* (Salt Lake City: Deseret Book, 1988), 177.

May 1: Thomas E. Cheney, *The Golden Legacy* (Layton: Peregrine Smith, 1974), 105.

May 2: Francis M. Gibbons, *David O. McKay: Apostle to the World, Prophet of God* (Salt Lake City: Deseret Book, 1986), 11.

May 3: Thomas E. Cheney, *The Golden Legacy* (Layton: Peregrine Smith, 1974), 109.

May 4: Michaelene P. Grassli, address at "Behold Your Little Ones," Churchwide satellite broadcast, January 23, 1994; reprinted in *Ensign*, April 1994, 62.

May 5: Thomas E. Cheney, *The Golden Legacy* (Layton: Peregrine Smith, 1974), 121.

May 6: Personal records of the author.

May 7: J. Randolph Ayre, *Illustrations to Inspire* (Salt Lake City: Bookcraft, 1968), 25.

May 8: Thomas E. Cheney, *The Golden Legacy* (Layton: Peregrine Smith, 1974), 131.

May 9: James E. Faust, general conference address, April 1, 1979; reprinted in *Ensign*, May 1979, 53.

May 10: Joseph F. McConkie, *True and Faithful* (Salt Lake City: Bookcraft, 1971), 19–20.

May 11: Edward L. Kimball and Andrew E. Kimball Jr., *Spencer W. Kimball* (Salt Lake City: Bookcraft, 1977), 416.

May 12: Matthew Cowley, *Matthew Cowley Speaks* (Salt Lake City: Deseret Book, 1976), 243.

May 13: Marion G. Romney, general conference address, March 31, 1979; reprinted in *Ensign,* May 1979, 41.

May 14: Edward L. Kimball and Andrew E. Kimball Jr., *Spencer W. Kimball* (Salt Lake City: Bookcraft, 1977), 233.

May 15: Alma Heaton, *Attention-Getters and Forfeits* (Salt Lake City: Bookcraft, 1972), 30.

May 16: "News of the Church," *Ensign,* September 1973, 86.

May 17: *This People,* April 1985, 22.

May 18: Edward L. Kimball, ed., *The Writings of Camilla Eyring Kimball* (Salt Lake City: Deseret Book, 1988), 104; Marvin J. Ashton quote in *Ensign,* November 1981, 90 (as quoted in *LDS Speakers Sourcebook,* Aspen Press, 1991, 487).

May 19: Chieko N. Okazaki, *Aloha!* (Salt Lake City: Deseret Book, 1995), 77.

May 20: Leon R. Hartshorn, *Outstanding Stories by General Authorities, Volume III* (Salt Lake City: Deseret Book, 1974), 65.

May 21: Jeanne Woolfenden, "There's Always the Promise of Morning," *New Era,* May 1977, 28.

· Sources ·

May 22: Hugh B. Brown, *An Abundant Life: The Memoirs of Hugh B. Brown* (Salt Lake City: Signature, 1988), 3.

May 23: "Daughters-in-Law Share Memories of 'Dad,'" *Church News,* March 11, 1995, 16.

May 24: Elaine Cannon, general women's meeting address, March 27, 1982; reprinted in *Ensign,* May 1982, 95.

May 25: Kimball, Smith, Ashton, et al., *Joy* (Salt Lake City: Deseret Book, 1980), 134.

May 26: Stephen Webster, "This Is the Place," *Las Vegas Latter-day Family Journal,* September 21, 1988, 2.

May 27: Ann Edwards Cannon, "The Luckiest Girl Around," *New Era,* November 1981, 10.

May 28: Richard S. Van Wagoner and Steven C. Walker, *A Book of Mormons* (Salt Lake City: Signature, 1982), 50.

May 29: Marvin J. Ashton, *Ye Are My Friends* (Salt Lake City: Deseret Book, 1982), 100.

May 30: Richard S. Van Wagoner and Steven C. Walker, *A Book of Mormons* (Salt Lake City: Signature, 1982), 100.

May 31: Richard S. Van Wagoner and Steven C. Walker, *A Book of Mormons* (Salt Lake City: Signature, 1982), 103.

Jun 1: Chieko N. Okazaki, *Aloha!* (Salt Lake City: Deseret Book, 1995), 39.

Jun 2: Kimball, Tanner, Romney, et al., *Prayer* (Salt Lake City: Deseret Book, 1977), 87.

Jun 3: Leonard J. Arrington and Susan Arrington Madsen, *Sunbonnet Sisters* (Salt Lake City: Bookcraft, 1984), 132.

Jun 4: "Associate Remembers Good Times, Quick Wit of Dear Friend, Neighbor," *Church News,* March 11, 1995, 19.

Jun 5: Joe J. Christensen, "Resolutions" from "Speaking Today," in *Ensign,* December 1994, 65.

Jun 6: Personal records of the author.

Jun 7: Vaughn J. Featherstone, *Commitment* (Salt Lake City: Bookcraft, 1982), 40.

Jun 8: Bryant S. Hinckley, *That Ye Might Have Joy* (Salt Lake City: Bookcraft, 1958), 111.

Jun 9: Harold B. Lee quote in *Ensign,* January 1974, 23 (as quoted in *LDS Speakers Sourcebook,* Aspen Press, 1991, 352).

Jun 10: Hugh B. Brown, *An Abundant Life: The Memoirs of Hugh B. Brown* (Salt Lake City: Signature, 1988), 71.

Jun 11: Matthew Cowley, *Matthew Cowley Speaks* (Salt Lake City: Deseret Book, 1976), 356.

Jun 12: Lorenzo Snow quote in *LDS Speakers Sourcebook,* Aspen Press, 1991, 168.

Jun 13: Bonnie D. Parkin, general young women's conference address, March 25, 1995.

· SOURCES ·

Jun 14: Hugh B. Brown, *An Abundant Life: The Memoirs of Hugh B. Brown* (Salt Lake City: Signature, 1988), 89.

Jun 15: Thomas E. Cheney, *The Golden Legacy* (Layton: Peregrine Smith, 1974), 27.

Jun 16: Chieko N. Okazaki, *Aloha!* (Salt Lake City: Deseret Book, 1995), 41.

Jun 17: James E. Faust, "The Way of an Eagle" *Ensign*, August 1994, 6.

Jun 18: Matthew Cowley, *Matthew Cowley Speaks* (Salt Lake City: Deseret Book, 1976), 3, 5, 248.

Jun 19: Personal records of the author.

Jun 20: *Sports Illustrated*, February 6, 1995, 38.

Jun 21: Leonard J. Arrington and Susan Arrington Madsen, *Sunbonnet Sisters* (Salt Lake City: Bookcraft, 1984), 13–15.

Jun 22: Leonard J. Arrington and Susan Arrington Madsen, *Sunbonnet Sisters* (Salt Lake City: Bookcraft, 1984), 17.

Jun 23: Emerson Roy West, *Profiles of the Presidents* (Salt Lake City: Deseret Book, 1980), 229.

Jun 24: Personal records of the author.

Jun 25: Richard S. Van Wagoner and Steven C. Walker, *A Book of Mormons* (Salt Lake City: Signature, 1982), 273.

Jun 26: Janet G. Lee, "Choices and Challenges," *Ensign*, February 1995, 59.

Jun 27: Vaughn J. Featherstone, general conference address, October 1, 1983; reprinted in *Ensign,* November 1983, 37.

Jun 28: Brad Rock, *Deseret News,* April 13, 1995, D–2.

Jun 29: Kimball, Tanner, Romney, et al., *Prayer* (Salt Lake City: Deseret Book, 1977), 130.

Jun 30: Jacob de Jager, general conference address, April 3, 1983; reprinted in *Ensign,* May 1983, 75.

Jul 1: Wm. Grant Bangerter, general conference address, October 2, 1988; reprinted in *Ensign,* November 1985, 81.

Jul 2: Personal records of the author.

Jul 3: Leonard J. Arrington, "Missionaries in Church History," *New Era,* June 1973, 65.

Jul 4: Edward L. Kimball and Andrew E. Kimball Jr., *Spencer W. Kimball* (Salt Lake City: Bookcraft, 1977), 419.

Jul 5: Leon R. Hartshorn, *Classic Stories from the Lives of Our Prophets* (Salt Lake City: Deseret Book, 1975), 349.

Jul 6: Matthew Cowley, *Matthew Cowley Speaks* (Salt Lake City: Deseret Book, 1976), 176.

Jul 7: Marvin J. Ashton, general conference address, April 6, 1985; reprinted in *Ensign,* May 1985, 44.

Jul 8: Marion G. Romney, general conference address, October 2, 1976; reprinted in *Ensign*, November 1976, 123.

Jul 9: Vaughn J. Featherstone, *Commitment* (Salt Lake City: Bookcraft, 1982), 41.

Jul 10: Edward L. Kimball, ed., *The Writings of Camilla Eyring Kimball* (Salt Lake City: Deseret Book, 1988), 137; George Q. Morris quote in *Conference Report,* April 1952, 31 (as quoted in *LDS Speakers Sourcebook,* Aspen Press, 1992, 12).

Jul 11: Leon R. Hartshorn, *Remarkable Stories from the Lives of Latter-day Saint Women* (Randall Book Company, 1973), 215.

Jul 12: Victor L. Brown, general conference address, April 3, 1982; reprinted in *Ensign*, May 1982, 34.

Jul 13: Matthew Cowley, "Miracles," *New Era,* June 1975, 39.

Jul 14: Leon R. Hartshorn, *Remarkable Stories from the Lives of Latter-day Saint Women* (Randall Book Company, 1973), 242–43.

Jul 15: Joseph F. McConkie, *True and Faithful* (Salt Lake City: Bookcraft, 1971), 74, 77.

Jul 16: Sterling W. Sill, general conference address; reprinted in *Ensign*, June 1971, 43.

Jul 17: Robert E. Wells, "Faking It and the Fourth French Horn," *New Era,* April 1977, 6.

· SOURCES ·

Jul 18: Clifton Fadiman, ed., *The Little, Brown Book of Anecdotes* (New York: Little, Brown, and Company, 1985), 360.

Jul 19: G. Homer Durham, *N. Eldon Tanner: His Life and Service* (Salt Lake City: Deseret Book, 1982), 10.

Jul 20: Leon R. Hartshorn, *Remarkable Stories from the Lives of Latter-day Saint Women* (Randall Book Company, 1973), 159–60.

Jul 21: G. Homer Durham, *N. Eldon Tanner: His Life and Service* (Salt Lake City: Deseret Book, 1982), 96.

Jul 22: Joseph F. McConkie, *True and Faithful* (Salt Lake City: Bookcraft, 1971), 73.

Jul 23: G. Homer Durham, *N. Eldon Tanner: His Life and Service* (Salt Lake City: Deseret Book, 1982), 213–14.

Jul 24: J. Reuben Clark quote, *Church News,* June 14, 1969 (as quoted in *LDS Speakers Sourcebook,* Aspen Press, 1991, 169).

Jul 25: Chieko N. Okazaki, *Aloha!* (Salt Lake City: Deseret Book, 1995), 59.

Jul 26: G. Homer Durham, *N. Eldon Tanner: His Life and Service* (Salt Lake City: Deseret Book, 1982), 302–303.

Jul 27: Sterling W. Sill, *The Laws of Success* (Salt Lake City: Deseret Book, 1975), 169.

Jul 28: Matthew Cowley, *Matthew Cowley Speaks* (Salt Lake City: Deseret Book, 1976), 133.

Jul 29: Eleanor Knowles, *Howard W. Hunter* (Salt Lake City: Deseret Book, 1994), 282.

Jul 30: Hugh B. Brown, *An Abundant Life: The Memoirs of Hugh B. Brown* (Salt Lake City: Signature, 1988), 143–44.

Jul 31: H. Burke Peterson, general conference address, April 7, 1985; reprinted in *Ensign,* May 1985, 65.

Aug 1: Heber J. Grant, *Gospel Standards,* an Improvement Era publication, 1942, 62–63.

Aug 2: David B. Haight, general conference address, April 4, 1981; reprinted in *Ensign,* May 1981, 42.

Aug 3: Personal records of the author, letter dated February 6, 1978.

Aug 4: Joe J. Christensen, general conference address, April 2, 1995; reprinted in the *Ensign,* May 1995, 65.

Aug 5: James O. Mason, "Traveling with a Missionary Prophet," *New Era,* October 1977, 6.

Aug 6: Gene Allred Sessions, *Latter-day Patriots* (Salt Lake City: Deseret Book, 1975), 82–83.

Aug 7: Emerson Roy West, *Profiles of the Presidents* (Salt Lake City: Deseret Book, 1980), 203–204.

· Sources ·

Aug 8: Francis M. Gibbons, *David O. McKay: Apostle to the World, Prophet of God* (Salt Lake City: Deseret Book, 1986), 232–33.

Aug 9: Benson, Hinckley, Packer, et al., *Love* (Salt Lake City: Deseret Book, 1986), 44.

Aug 10: *Supporting Saints* (a compilation of life stories of nineteenth century Mormons), Religious Studies Center, BYU, 1985, 59.

Aug 11: "David O. McKay: The Worth of a Soul," *New Era,* January 1972, 60.

Aug 12: Thomas E. Cheney, *The Golden Legacy* (Layton: Peregrine Smith, 1974), 121.

Aug 13: Leon R. Hartshorn, *Exceptional Stories from the Lives of Our Apostles* (Salt Lake City: Deseret Book, 1972), 46.

Aug 14: Leon R. Hartshorn, *Exceptional Stories from the Lives of Our Apostles* (Salt Lake City: Deseret Book, 1972), 71.

Aug 15: Mikal and Ilene Lofgren, *Salt: Humor and Wisdom from Brigham Young* (Salt Lake City: Moth House Publications, 1979), 71.

Aug 16: *Supporting Saints* (a compilation of life stories of nineteenth century Mormons), Religious Studies Center, BYU, 1985, 240.

Aug 17: William B. Smart, "President Joseph Fielding Smith: A Tithing Child," *New Era,* August 1972, 6.

Aug 18: Leon R. Hartshorn, *Classic Stories from the Lives of Our Prophets* (Salt Lake City: Deseret Book, 1975), 10.

Aug 19: Thomas E. Cheney, *The Golden Legacy* (Layton: Peregrine Smith, 1974), 41.

Aug 20: Personal records of the author, letter dated February 6, 1978.

Aug 21: "President Hunter Was Calm, Positive amid Stressful and Perilous Situation," *Church News,* March 11, 1995, 19.

Aug 22: Matthew Cowley, *Matthew Cowley Speaks* (Salt Lake City: Deseret Book, 1976), 220.

Aug 23: Gene Allred Sessions, *Latter-day Patriots* (Salt Lake City: Deseret Book, 1975), 83.

Aug 24: Richard L. Evans, general conference address, October 1, 1971; reprinted in *Ensign,* December 1971, 57. Sterling W. Sill, general conference address, October 1, 1971; reprinted in *Ensign,* December 1971, 93.

Aug 25: Gene Allred Sessions, *Latter-day Patriots* (Salt Lake City: Deseret Book, 1975), 184.

Aug 26: Maurine Jensen Ward, "General Authorities Wives: Sister Zina Young Card Brown," *New Era,* July 1994, 38.

Aug 27: Sterling W. Sill, "The Convert," *New Era,* February 1973, 44.

Aug 28: Sheri L. Dew, *Sharlene Wells, Miss America* (Salt Lake City: Deseret Book, 1985), 9.

· Sources ·

Aug 29: Leonard J. Arrington, "Missionaries in Church History," *New Era*, June 1973, 65.

Aug 30: Clifton Fadiman, ed., *The Little, Brown Book of Anecdotes* (New York: Little, Brown, and Company, 1985), 554.

Aug 31: Leon R. Hartshorn, *Exceptional Stories from the Lives of Our Apostles* (Salt Lake City: Deseret Book, 1972), 149–50.

Sep 1: Francis M. Gibbons, *David O. McKay: Apostle to the World, Prophet of God* (Salt Lake City: Deseret Book, 1986), 102–103.

Sep 2: LeGrand Richards, "Patriarchal Blessings," *New Era*, February 1977.

Sep 3: Rex D. Pinegar, general conference address, October 2, 1994; reprinted in *Ensign*, November 1994, 82.

Sep 4: *Woman to Woman: Selected Talks from the BYU Women's Conferences* (Salt Lake City: Deseret Book, 1986), 25.

Sep 5: Chieko N. Okazaki, *Lighten Up!* (Salt Lake City: Deseret Book, 1993), 148–49.

Sep 6: LaVell Edwards with Lee Benson, *LaVell: Airing It Out* (Salt Lake City: Shadow Mountain, 1995), 165.

Sep 7: Bruce R. McConkie, "Agency or Inspiration?" *New Era*, January 1975, 38.

Sep 8: Marion G. Romney, "Discovering the Book of Mormon," *New Era*, May 1975, 5.

· Sources ·

Sep 9: "Daughters-in-Law Share Memories of 'Dad,'" *Church News,* March 11, 1995, 16.

Sep 10: Sterling W. Sill, *The Laws of Success* (Salt Lake City: Deseret Book, 1975), 68.

Sep 11: Hugh B. Brown, *An Abundant Life: The Memoirs of Hugh B. Brown* (Salt Lake City: Signature, 1988), 2–3.

Sep 12: George Durrant, *Look at the Sky* (Salt Lake City: Bookcraft, 1994), 1.

Sep 13: "David O. McKay: The Worth of a Soul," *New Era,* January 1972, 59.

Sep 14: Lucile C. Tate, *LeGrand Richards: Beloved Apostle* (Salt Lake City: Bookcraft, 1982), 280.

Sep 15: Leon R. Hartshorn, *Outstanding Stories by General Authorities, Volume II* (Salt Lake City: Deseret Book, 1974), 211.

Sep 16: Chieko N. Okazaki, *Lighten Up!* (Salt Lake City: Deseret Book, 1993), 152.

Sep 17: Max Nolan, "J. Golden Kimball in the South," *New Era,* July 1985, 7.

Sep 18: Susan Arrington Madsen, *The Lord Needed a Prophet* (Salt Lake City: Deseret Book, 1990), 26.

Sep 19: Leon R. Hartshorn, *Classic Stories from the Lives of Our Prophets* (Salt Lake City: Deseret Book, 1988), 135.

Sep 20: Emerson Roy West, *Profiles of the Presidents* (Salt Lake City: Deseret Book, 1980), 251.

Sep 21: Editor's Note, *This People,* December 1985/January 1986, 7.

Sep 22: Elaine Cannon, "Voices," *New Era,* July 1980, 16.

Sep 23: Ann Edwards Cannon, "The Luckiest Girl Around," *New Era,* November 1981, 10.

Sep 24: Leon R. Hartshorn, *Outstanding Stories by General Authorities, Volume III* (Salt Lake City: Deseret Book, 1974), 11.

Sep 25: "Lengthening His Stride," insert in *New Era,* December 1985.

Sep 26: Elaine Cannon, "Voices," *New Era,* July 1980, 13–14.

Sep 27: Richard S. Van Wagoner and Steven C. Walker, *A Book of Mormons* (Salt Lake City: Signature, 1982), 100.

Sep 28: Benson, Hinckley, Packer, et al., *Love* (Salt Lake City: Deseret Book, 1986), 41–42.

Sep 29: J. Randolph Ayre, *Illustrations to Inspire* (Salt Lake City: Bookcraft, 1968), 83.

Sep 30: Personal records of the author.

Oct 1: "President N. Eldon Tanner: Lifter, Builder, Leader," *New Era,* February 1983, 15.

Oct 2: D. Arthur Haycock and Heidi S. Swinton, *In the Company of Prophets* (Salt Lake City: Deseret Book, 1993), 62.

· Sources ·

Oct 3: Leon R. Hartshorn, *Classic Stories from the Lives of Our Prophets* (Salt Lake City: Deseret Book, 1971), 196.

Oct 4: Leon R. Hartshorn, *Classic Stories from the Lives of Our Prophets* (Salt Lake City: Deseret Book, 1988), 299.

Oct 5: Teddy E. Brewerton, general conference address, April 5, 1981; reprinted in *Ensign,* May 1981, 69.

Oct 6: Personal records of the author.

Oct 7: Marvin J. Ashton, *Ye Are My Friends* (Salt Lake City: Deseret Book, 1982), 22.

Oct 8: David O. McKay, address to employees of the Physical Facilities Department of the Church, Hotel Utah, 1965 (as quoted in *LDS Speakers Sourcebook,* Aspen Press, 1991, 460).

Oct 9: Personal records of the author.

Oct 10: George Durrant, *Look at the Sky* (Salt Lake City: Bookcraft, 1994), 2.

Oct 11: Heber J. Grant, *Gospel Standards,* an Improvement Era publication, 1942, 99.

Oct 12: Heber J. Grant, *Gospel Standards,* an Improvement Era publication, 1942, 114.

Oct 13: Heber J. Grant, *Gospel Standards,* an Improvement Era publication, 1942, 242.

Oct 14: Matthew Cowley, *Matthew Cowley Speaks* (Salt Lake City: Deseret Book, 1976), 69.

Oct 15: Robert L. Simpson, "I Broke the Quarterback's Finger," *Ensign,* January 1977, 83.

Oct 16: Leon R. Hartshorn, *Outstanding Stories by General Authorities, Volume II* (Salt Lake City: Deseret Book, 1974), 73.

Oct 17: Leon R. Hartshorn, *Classic Stories from the Lives of Our Prophets* (Salt Lake City: Deseret Book, 1975), 280–81.

Oct 18: Thomas E. Cheney, *The Golden Legacy* (Layton: Peregrine Smith, 1974), 44.

Oct 19: Kimball, Smith, Ashton, et al., *Joy* (Salt Lake City: Deseret Book, 1980), 177.

Oct 20: Leon R. Hartshorn, *Classic Stories from the Lives of Our Prophets* (Salt Lake City: Deseret Book, 1975), 13.

Oct 21: *This People,* April 1985, 30.

Oct 22: Ann Edwards Cannon, "The Luckiest Girl Around," *New Era,* November 1981, 10.

Oct 23: J. Randolph Ayre, *Illustrations to Inspire* (Salt Lake City: Bookcraft, 1968), 68.

Oct 24: Lyman Wight "History," MS 27 (1865), 457.

Oct 25: Personal records of the author.

Oct 26: Clifton Fadiman, ed., *The Little, Brown Book of Anecdotes* (New York: Little, Brown, and Company, 1985), 360.

· SOURCES ·

Oct 27: Edward L. Kimball, ed., *The Writings of Camilla Eyring Kimball* (Salt Lake City: Deseret Book, 1988), xiv, xv.

Oct 28: Clarissa Young Spencer, *Brigham Young at Home* (Salt Lake City: Deseret Book, 1972), 140.

Oct 29: Mary Ellen Edmunds, *Love Is a Verb* (Salt Lake City: Deseret Book, 1995), 30, 31.

Oct 30: Hugh B. Brown, *An Abundant Life: The Memoirs of Hugh B. Brown* (Salt Lake City: Signature, 1988), 53.

Oct 31: Personal records of the author.

Nov 1: Clarissa Young Spencer, *Brigham Young at Home* (Salt Lake City: Deseret Book, 1972), 151.

Nov 2: Personal records of the author.

Nov 3: J. Richard Clarke, general conference address, April 3, 1982; reprinted in *Ensign,* May 1982, 77.

Nov 4: H. David Burton, general conference address, April 13, 1994; reprinted in *Ensign,* May 1994, 68.

Nov 5: Victor L. Brown, general conference address, April 6, 1985; reprinted in *Ensign,* May 1985, 14.

Nov 6: Caroline Eyring Miner and Edward L. Kimball, *Camilla* (Salt Lake City: Deseret Book, 1980), 182–83.

· Sources ·

Nov 7: Vaughn J. Featherstone, general conference address, October 3, 1987; reprinted in *Ensign,* November 1987, 27.

Nov 8: David O. McKay quote in *Conference Report,* 60, October 1967 (as quoted in *LDS Speakers Sourcebook,* Aspen Press, 1991, 208).

Nov 9: Marlin K. Jensen, general conference address, April 2, 1994; in *Ensign,* May 1994, 48.

Nov 10: "Manti Grew amid Struggles and Surprises," *Deseret News,* March 21, 1995, B–3.

Nov 11: Kathleen Fox, "Family Courts," *Ensign,* January 1995, 65.

Nov 12: Kimball, Smith, Ashton, et al., *Joy* (Salt Lake City: Deseret Book, 1980), 92.

Nov 13: Richard S. Van Wagoner and Steven C. Walker, *A Book of Mormons* (Salt Lake City: Signature, 1982), 39.

Nov 14: Dallin H. Oaks, general conference address, April 2, 1994; reprinted in *Ensign,* May 1994, 35.

Nov 15: Marion G. Romney, general conference address, April 3, 1971; reprinted in *Ensign,* June 1971, 35.

Nov 16: Personal records of the author.

Nov 17: John R. Lasater, general conference address, April 3, 1988; reprinted in *Ensign,* May 1988, 74.

Nov 18: G. Homer Durham, *N. Eldon Tanner: His Life and Service* (Salt Lake City: Deseret Book, 1982), 112.

Nov 19: Thomas E. Cheney, *The Golden Legacy* (Layton: Peregrine Smith, 1974), 91, 100.

Nov 20: Clifton Fadiman, ed., *The Little, Brown Book of Anecdotes* (New York: Little, Brown, and Company, 1985), 197; Sterling W. Sill quote in *The Laws of Success,* Deseret Book, 1975, 93.

Nov 21: *Supporting Saints* (a compilation of life stories of 19th century Mormons), Religious Studies Center, BYU, 1985, 57.

Nov 22: Marvin J. Ashton, *Ye Are My Friends* (Salt Lake City: Deseret Book, 1982), 60–61.

Nov 23: "President Joseph Fielding Smith: Student of the Gospel," *New Era,* January 1972, 64.

Nov 24: Teddy E. Brewerton, general conference address, April 5, 1981; reprinted in *Ensign,* May 1981, 70.

Nov 25: D. Arthur Haycock and Heidi S. Swinton, *In the Company of Prophets* (Salt Lake City: Deseret Book, 1993), 21.

Nov 26: N. Eldon Tanner's quote in *LDS Speakers Sourcebook,* Aspen Press, 1991, 481.

Nov 27: Personal records of the author.

Nov 28: Joe J. Christensen, general conference address, April 2, 1995; reprinted in *Ensign,* May 1995, 64.

Nov 29: Personal records of the author.

Nov 30: Thomas E. Cheney, *The Golden Legacy* (Layton: Peregrine Smith, 1974), 70.

Dec 1: G. Homer Durham, *N. Eldon Tanner: His Life and Service* (Salt Lake City: Deseret Book, 1982), 44.

Dec 2: Bryant S. Hinckley, *That Ye Might Have Joy* (Salt Lake City: Bookcraft, 1958), 121.

Dec 3: *This People,* August/September 1985, 53.

Dec 4: Matthew Cowley, *Matthew Cowley Speaks* (Salt Lake City: Deseret Book, 1976), 248.

Dec 5: Marvin J. Ashton, *Ye Are My Friends* (Salt Lake City: Deseret Book, 1982), 108.

Dec 6: Mikal and Ilene Lofgren, *Salt: Humor and Wisdom from Brigham Young* (Salt Lake City: Moth House Publications, 1979), 76.

Dec 7: Lucile C. Tate, *LeGrand Richards: Beloved Apostle* (Salt Lake City: Bookcraft, 1982), 18.

Dec 8: Vaughn J. Featherstone, general conference address, October 1, 1983; reprinted in *Ensign,* November 1983, 36.

Dec 9: Personal records of the author, letter dated February 6, 1978.

Dec 10: Ezra Taft Benson, general conference address, October 1, 1977; reprinted in *Ensign,* November 1977, 31.

• Sources •

Dec 11: Robert D. Hales, general conference address, April 6, 1985; reprinted in *Ensign*, May 1985, 29.

Dec 12: Marvin J. Ashton's quote in *Ensign*, November 1976 (as quoted in *LDS Speakers Sourcebook*, Aspen Press, 1991, 526).

Dec 13: Personal records of the author.

Dec 14: Lucy Gertsch Thomson, *Stories That Live* (Salt Lake City: Deseret Book, 1956), 16–17.

Dec 15: Personal records of the author.

Dec 16: Mikal and Ilene Lofgren, *Salt: Humor and Wisdom from Brigham Young* (Salt Lake City: Moth House Publications, 1979), 91.

Dec 17: N. Eldon Tanner, general conference address, October 1982; reprinted in *Ensign*, November 1982, 82.

Dec 18: Ardeth Greene Kapp, *My Neighbor, My Sister, My Friend* (Salt Lake City: Deseret Book, 1990), 141.

Dec 19: Matthew Cowley, *Matthew Cowley Speaks* (Salt Lake City: Deseret Book, 1976), 133, 237.

Dec 20: Richard S. Van Wagoner and Steven C. Walker, *A Book of Mormons* (Salt Lake City: Signature, 1982), 307.

Dec 21: G. Homer Durham, *N. Eldon Tanner: His Life and Service* (Salt Lake City: Deseret Book, 1982), 286.

· Sources ·

Dec 22: Richard S. Van Wagoner and Steven C. Walker, *A Book of Mormons* (Salt Lake City: Signature, 1982), 347.

Dec 23: Vaughn J. Featherstone, general conference address, October 1, 1983; reprinted in *Ensign*, November 1983, 36.

Dec 24: Orson F. Whitney, general conference address, April 4, 1926; reprinted in *Conference Report*, 31.

Dec 25: Elaine L. Jack, *Eye to Eye, Heart to Heart* (Salt Lake City: Deseret Book, 1992), 172.

Dec 26: Linda and Richard Eyre, *Teaching Your Children Values* (New York: Simon & Schuster, 1993), 31.

Dec 27: Leon R. Hartshorn, *Remarkable Stories from the Lives of Latter-day Saint Women* (Salt Lake City: Deseret Book, 1975), 178.

Dec 28: Francis M. Gibbons, *David O. McKay: Apostle to the World, Prophet of God* (Salt Lake City: Deseret Book, 1986), 18–19.

Dec 29: Alma Heaton, *Attention-Getters and Forfeits* (Salt Lake City: Bookcraft, 1972), 22.

Dec 30: Derek A. Cuthbert, "The Futility of Fear," *New Era*, November 1985, 49.

Dec 31: Marion G. Romney, general conference address, October 1982; reprinted in *Ensign*, November 1982, 91.

· INDEX ·

RICHARD NASH, a graduate of the University of Utah, works as public relations manager of LDS Hospital. His experience includes newspaper reporting, advertising, and speechwriting for business, political, and health care leaders.

Richard lives in Salt Lake City with his wife, Laurie, and their three children. He serves as a bishop in the LDS church.

· DO YOU HAVE A STORY? ·

If you have a humorous or touching LDS story, thought, or anecdote—and you'd like to see it included in a possible sequel to *Lengthen Your Smile*—please send a copy of your story and your name, address, and telephone number to:

> *Lengthen Your Smile*
> 2798 Wilshire Drive
> Salt Lake City, UT 84109

The author will contact you if he decides to use your submission.